AN AUTOBIOGRAPHY WITH SECRECY

HOW I VALUE MYSELF

STEVEWEALTH FIRENEW

I would prefer to make mention of some special and well-meaning personalities as those to whom I would dedicate this book, 'An Autobiography with Secrecy' to. However, it is importunate to ascribe a thoughtful dedication first and foremost to 'The Invisible GOD' from Whom I came to exist:

My Creator:

The LORD of the Spirits has been my Maker because He formed and fashioned me; my Provider because He feeds me satisfactorily everyday; my Guard because He protects me always from the evil one; and He has been my Guide because He directs and leads me all the times on the paths of righteousness for sake of His Name.

The unseen Man Who has been longer before now than I was born, known me originally, therefore, I dedicate this unique book to Him.

Without His presence around my life, I would not have been available to bring this book into fruition.

My Selfless, Biological Parents:

Mrs. Happy Esther A. Ocloo-Fianu has been my lovely, sweet, selfless, biological mother ever since she conceived me in her womb.

I love her for the maximum care, admonishments and love that she has hitherto showered on me whenever she had the privilege to do so.

She has for several years been to me like the best Girlfriend that I never had yet, I do hope and expect to have and keep a beautiful, wonderful but selfless lady.

Late Reverend Captain David Kodjo Oye Fianu of blessed memory had been my selfless, biological father, mentor and teacher, while he walked the shores of this terrestrial plane and did the work of the Lord Jesus Christ for several decades until he bit the dust in the most perfect peace and without his being available here on the Earth, GOD would not have permitted me to appear here on the Earth.

Owing to this, I do love him extremely, and he will interminably remain in the deepest parts of my retentive memory.

My Three Beautiful Sisters:

Mrs. Precious-Abigail Thompson, Belgium.

Mrs. Janet Selassie Anum, Ghana.

Mrs. Catherine D. Boateng, Ghana.

They all have played their respective, individual purposes and roles in my life in order to allow me to make it now.

My Responsible Brothers-In-Law:

Mr. Alexander A. Thompson; he is that wonderful and caring man who took care of me for almost the most years of my life, which amounts to fifteen years.

Mr. Benjamin A. Anum; he is that man who played a vital role in making me realize my musical potentials.

Mr. Charles Boateng; he is that hospitable man, who is ever willing to accommodate anyone who beckons him and he always cares enough about everyone in the extended family.

These have been my almost, perfect brothers for over a couple of decades and have also, played some special roles in my life one way or another; and the unique love that one exhibited, another did for me in their own acceptable ways.

My Lovely Children:

Ernestina---She has been my premier, royal lady and princess.

Christabel---She follows suit in the challenge of royalty as my lady and princess.

Erica---She has been my remotest, country-side lady and princess.

Sandra---She is my first dreadlocked, born-girl and princess.

Celestine---She is my second dreadlocked, born-girl and princess.

Alexandrite-Abigail---She is my first albinoid princess.

Jerry-Nick---He is my second albinoid prince.

Prince Lord-Reigner---He will be my royal-blooded ruler.

My Gorgeous Queens:

Celestine---She has been helpful to me as my older queen in many ways.

Mercy---She has been helpful to two of my children with her as my lady but has been distant from me.

Gifty---She has been my queen and partner through thick and thin before I made it.

Cassandra---She has been my first beautiful damsel and princess.

Priscilla---She has been my first distant, dark damsel and princess.

Doris---She has been my second distant, dark, pretty damsel and princess.

My Friends:

I would like to dedicate this book to the following wonderful friends here;

my wonderful friend, Felix at Christson Gallery, Eric D, Enoch, Jake M, Gideon B, Nana Twum, Lawerh, Abeiku B, Bernard, Benjamin, Seth and many others who took care of me and who also spent time with me.

My Benefactor:

I do not want to forfeit the memory of Mr & Mrs Maxwell Asare, an amazing couple who reside in Tema Community 16. Almost a year ago, these wonderful individuals were charitable enough to offer me their two-bedroom apartment just to make sure that I have a roof over my head. I appreciate your sundry efforts in helping and supporting me for over twelve months.

Finally, I have reserved a special place in my heart and soul in order to thank and appreciate the efforts of everyone who matters in my life. I love you all!

Contents

Foreword

Apostle Dr John Duncan-Zuta

Having known Stevewealth for over four decades I would state that the content of his book has proven to me on the basis of what he has told me on several occasions about the mystery of some experiences that he had been through.

Anyways, Stevewealth Firenew is my son because, he is the only son of my maternally, related elder brother in respect of my mother. I have every right traditionally and by a great sense of family relationship to call him my son.

This book is indeed, "An Autobiography with Secrecy" on the part of my son, brother and above all my friend. This book contains loads of mysteries and secrecies from its beginning but not so towards its ending.

I have learnt a lot of things from him, for most of what I have gained in life owes all to the humble but great author of this wonderful book.

I am interminably indebted to God for such a wonderful, amazing and great individual like Steve in respect of everything as well as for the fruition of this book.

I do expect that with the content of this book as one which unveils a huge amount of mysterious facts coupled with his experiences, as far as his personal life is brought to bare.

The world is almost ready to meet the next bestseller in view of the author of this book, who is full of wisdom.

In his simplicity, no other individual is able to see and know what he is made up of and of what exactly he is worth.

I would like to state that he will explain perhaps in details the mystery which he has been shown or told, whether or not in visions or dreams or trances, as far as his experiences are concerned.

I cannot wait to see the rest of the world read this great masterpiece, for indeed, it is 'An Autobiography with Secrecy" with Stevewealth Firenew. Please do buy a copy of this book from the several online stores across the globe such as Amazon.com, Amazon.in, Amazon.co.uk, Flipkart.com and the Author's International Publisher Notion Press in India.

You are always a great blessing and are most welcome!

Acknowledgements

I had presumed a train of thoughts on how a bestseller should be written but I was hugely wrong.

I realized that writing or publishing a book which has the relevant potential to become a bestseller requires many an evidential proof in order to prevail on the digital marketing terrain and platforms as an even all-time bestseller.

I consulted with a number of amazing personalities who in one way or another, could be of an immense assistance to me in order to appear as both a published author and a bestseller.

Having been helped time and time again, I would not like to swim in the oceans and seas of ingratitude towards those who spent their time, energy and resource to be of a huge help to me when I really knew that it was quite difficult and a hard time to come across help of any kind from the people around me.

The following is an enumeration of the people who have helped me immensely, therefore, I would like the mentioning of their names here to appear as an everlasting memorial, each time someone reads this book.

Nana Twum, a wonderful friend and mentored son of mine, who is resident at Spintex for, he is one of the several friends and sons that I am practically, indebted to. He was the one who published the manuscript for me as a book on Notion Press via online in view of self-publishing.

The most amazing of its appearance will be overwhelming when they themselves read this book to see their names being mentioned in this book.

I thank these wonderful individuals:

My grandmother, Late Prophetess Catherine Abui-Norvi Dakpoh of blessed memory, who nurtured, fed and educated me in the best international school, in order for me to acquire a solid and strong educational foundation until now. I extend my heartfelt appreciation to you, lovely Granny!

My mom, Happy Esther Ocloo-Fianu, who helped tirelessly and strained herself with prayers in order to see me prevail through successfully. Thank you, mom!

My elder sister, Mrs. Abigail Thompson, who has been my second mom for almost one and half decade. Thanks a bunch, my sweet and sexy-delicious, elder sister!

My brother-in-law, Mr. Alexander Ayoku Thompson, a unique man who devoted his time and gave his energy and money to sponsor me abroad but for certain mysterious occurrences I had to return to his utmost surprise.

My two lovely sisters, Jane and Kate, I appreciate your sundry efforts in helping and getting me this far through your God-given potentials. I want to thank you two dearly.

My Family & Friends:

Aside the special roles played in my life by the nuclear family of mine, the extended family has not been exempted in their respective, individual duties and responsibilities, as far as my life in the midst of them is highly concerned.

I must confess expressly that they like the nuclear family have done quite enough in bringing me this far, to the extent that the world has observed and realized my inherent potentials when it comes to being one of the great authors of the world.

To such family relatives who cared enough about me, I duly dedicate this book.

I love you extremely! My close friends Mr Kojo Koomson, Mr Lamidi, Mr John Sena Danso, Mr James

Akoto, Mr Stephen Dapaah, Bishop Samuel Agyei, Frank, Patrick, Stone and others who have been with me since childhood have offered amazing loads of sacrificial service to me, one way or another in order to make me a part and parcel of their wonderful lives.

Those who have ever been my classmates or course mates, I care about you all. Thanks!

CHAPTER ONE

MYSTERY & SECRECY

In order to let you know about the mystery or secrecy which has been kept in this special book, you got to comprehend the fact that this book is about "An Autobiography with Secrecy" and this is traceable to the secrecy and mystery of my life, personhood, character, experience and more, in view of the title of my book as you have read above. I would like to expatiate to you on what the English word "mystery"or "secrecy" means or is first.

What Is Mystery?

Mystery is simply a veiled, concealed, hidden and shrouded piece of information, which is quite important enough to bring to someone or a group of people, either their freedom, wealth or otherwise when it is told or revealed by the one who has kept it for many years.

Mystery is capable of opening many a closed door to someone or to a number of people in a community as well as those people living within a nation.

Mystery has the tendency to cause a servant to become a master and can lead a peasant to become a royal.

This happens when a servant has for several years been able to keep a vital piece of information from a community of people but told them only to bring about their freedom.

Mystery is something that is difficult or impossible to understand or explain yet, there is always a unique individual who is capable of unfolding it in clear explanations.

Mystery is simply a hidden piece of information which is relevant to a dynasty of royals or a kingdom of kings, princes and rulers.

Facts About Mysteries

Let us take a look at the following important facts about mysteries, in other words, secrets.

Mystery is a secret which is kept for many years but must be revealed to free a nation of citizens that have been kept in a huge bondage for many centuries.

Mystery is a veiled, privileged piece of information which belongs to a people who have been in power for many ages yet are not supposed to be and until one man who knows such a secret reveals it they still keep ruling.

Mystery is maybe held by almost everyone but, can be kept by only a few people.

Everyone may have a mystery around them.

It is not a must that everyone should have a mystery because, not everyone is actually, capable of keeping it.

It is good that everyone keeps one secret or the other for a secret is a mystery.

Never expose your personal secrets except for making money out of them or for the sake of something much better and higher when you expose them.

Always learn to keep secrets and those of others until an opportuned situation appears when they would be required by the elites and the rich and the royals.

It helps for a people to keep a secret or mystery because, it makes them appear special amongst many others who do not keep one at all.

Almost every country of the world has a mystery or secret and every leader or president of the world has a secret.

Europeans have a bunch of secrets just as much as Africans.

The Black Man does have many secrets more or less than the secrets of the White Man.

Each of the Color Race which is found in the respective parts of the world possesses many a mystery which makes them special as a race.

Moslems have secrets just as much as Christians do when it comes to their religion.

The Pope of the Roman Catholic Church has a secret that is just as much as greater or smaller than the secrets that the Presidents of the worlds keep in their tenures.

Mothers have secrets more or less than what Fathers keep; Sisters and Brothers cannot be left out of the keeping of secrets when it comes to their relationships with one another as well as each other.

Some children are capable of keeping secrets until they are of age to expose them.

I do not know the secrets which you have kept but I will never tell you mine except for making huge amounts of money out of them when necessary.

Most royal families of the world like the Royal Family of the United Kingdom and Ireland, the Royal Families of the Seven Emirates, the Royal Family of Saudi Arabia, the Royal Family of Brunei, the Royal Family of Ashantis, the Royal Family of the Anglos, in fact, the list is quite longer than ever imagined.

Most Russians have kept some secrets and the same have been observed by many Ukrainians.

If such great, wealthy and prominent royal families do not have secrets or mysteries they would have been exposed to many a shame, defeat and disrespect.

The Bible is replete with secrets and mysteries on many subjects and topics such as sexual intimacy, marriage, the love of God towards the nation of Israel and many more.

Humanity has secrets which have not been kept and cannot be hidden from divinity.

Divinity has many secrets and mysteries which have been kept from humanity before time had begun and will be kept forever.

If you are prudent enough then, please, do keep only the secrets which will lead you to prominence and can bring you wealth in every aspect of your life.

It is hugely obvious that most people have been fed on the secrets of others to the point where they once in a while try to threaten them to send into their personal, bank accounts some money in order for them to still keep those secrets which they know or have about them.

Most political parties of across the world hold at least one secret or the other of other opposing political parties and use such secrets against themselves when and where relevant in other to gain dominance, popularity or votes from the available masses.

Many kings and queens rule their territories and kingdoms in the name of the secrets they have kept about themselves and will keep such secrets forever in order to keep ruling.

There are reasons why many ethnic groups in my country hit at themselves; they keep hatred against themselves in the name of secrets.

Particular tribes and people do not feel the eagerness to intermarry with other tribes because of certain secrets and despite the presence of Christianity they still do not yearn to intermarry with them.

Men have many secrets kept by themselves for themselves for various reasons in their discretion.

I would like to point out emphatically that even God, our source of existence has kept myriads of secrets from the children of men.

It's the choice and will of God to reveal unto the sons of men, the ancient secrets of everything in creation.

God does so when He deems it fit for the descendants of Adam to be told of the secrets or hidden things in creation at a set time according to His will.

The issue of Godliness is a great mystery to all of humanity and can be known, understood by those who have been chosen by God for some special tasks regarding His Kingdom.

When God came to dwell amongst men, we did not realize His divinity amongst us until He ascended into the heaven of heavens through the thick clouds; for this has hitherto been a great secret as well as mystery to many Christians and believers.

Everything about divinity is a mystery to humanity yet it takes divinity for some of such secrets or mysteries to be unveiled to mankind.

Almost everything about humanity is shrouded in several mysteries to mankind however, it takes divinity for them to be told, revealed and known.

My Ten Commandments on Mysteries

The following are are some ten effective commandments on secrets or mysteries which have been of help to me personally and so in the name of legacy, I would like to bequeath them to you like a patriarch would to his posterity:

1. Never expose secrets to people which will not bring you honor, glory, power, money and fame.

2. Always keep those secrets which are capable of leading you into the state of honor, glory, power, money and fame.

3. Always eschew the tendency to expose either your personal secrets or those of others until, it is ever necessary to say them when you have consulted with them or they are dead and gone then, you can make money out of such secrets in order to become prominent.

4. Be careful of how you expose the serious secrets of others to the public.

5. Always keep the secrets of the nakedness of kings, presidents and the rich in order to live longer than you should.

6. Never threaten people with the secrets which you have kept about them. They might hire an assassin to wipe out your existence.

7. Always bear in mind that the foolish man is one who is quick to expose the secrets of others to the public.

8. Always bear in mind that the man who exposed the secrets of his king was the same who betrayed him.

9. Always keep secrets as a wise person.

10. Know for sure that it's easy to unearth a hidden treasure but quite difficult to unveil or reveal even a single mystery or secret.

The Mystery of Your Original Being

Before I begin to unveil your original self to you, I would like to tell you emphatically, that you are a God on this terrestrial plane over obstacles, circumstances and sin.

It is obvious that you may have read in the Bible or been told by many Christians that, Satan usurped your Earthly Kingdom in order to gain your power and dominion through our first parents Adam and Eve.

This is the reason why he, Satan or the Devil, has hitherto been seen or regarded as the god of this world in which you live.

Irrespective of this fact, I have got to submit to you that he has become the "God of this world" however, you are even now, have become the "God over he who has become the God of this world" in every way.

On this note here and now, I am divinely endorsed to tell you some mysteries about your original being or self because, this has been who you really were and are even now, before you were allowed to appear here on the Earth.

In Psalm 82:6, the LORD of the Spirits Himself intimated that, "...***Ye are 'Gods' and children of the Most High***..." And without realizing this truth you will die as mere mortals.

Hence, I would like to state here that, every human being living on this terrestrial plane called the Earth is originally divine, which makes you a God ruling in your kingdom in respect of the affairs of this Earth.

The Earth is one of the several, planetary bodies suspending within the physical universe. Again, originally Man is something else that is extremely powerful but is an 'Eternal Mind' or Spirit.

He therefore, before creation had shared eternity with the Supreme GOD as well as with the Gods and other Spirits who pre-existed before creation.

Men as Spirits were once resident in the Spiritual Universe prior to entering into this visible universe through the pre-ordained channels of their fathers whose willful or reluctant intentions had offered them up as spirits to those chosen women called their 'mothers' to be the predestined custodians of the secret doorways of both incarnation and reincarnation in order for us to be part and parcel of the existing living beings in nature.

We therefore, owe all our earthly parents a gigantic amount of indebtedness but prior to owing them such an extremely great indebtedness, we must acknowledge the fact and truth that there exists the LORD of the Spirits, Whose sole responsibility it was to permit every spirit to be presently available here on the Earth as a human.

To Him, the Supreme GOD, is the Ultimate Spirit, that all and sundry owe massive appreciations. Despite His being the LORD of all the Spirits, He has fully endorsed polytheism since time immemorial to be the practice for various traditions and religions in the world.

As a matter of fact, polytheism can be viewed in several 'isms' thus, monotheism, pantheism, henotheism among others. In view of this, we should not forget that this brings about the existent of 'The Gods' as regards the Hebrew word "Elohim".

The Bible from the beginning has revealed the existence of Elohim to mankind yet, has failed to state that Elohim in the original manuscripts refered to the pre-existent Deities that I would like to call here as 'The Gods'.

Therefore, 'The Gods' were the very Spirits Who were with the Supreme GOD when He had taken the initiative to make Man their 'image and likeness'. As nothing could be done to conceal further the truth, the Bible goes on to reveal this and I quote:

"***And God said, 'Let Us make Man in Our image and likeness***..." Genesis 1:26.

In my enlightened state I would write those words as such:

"And the Supreme GOD said to the Gods, 'Let Us (the Supreme GOD and the Gods altogether) make Man Our

(thus the Supreme GOD's and the Gods') image and likeness"

Man was not made in the image and likeness of the Supreme GOD and the Gods. Rather, He was directly made the image and likeness of Them. So then if there had not been the pre-existence of 'the Gods' with the Supreme GOD in respect of the Hebrew word 'Elohim', why then should the Bible use plural instead of singular?

The usage of the word 'Elohim' originally has proven that it took the Supreme GOD with the Gods to corporate in the creation of Man and to also, create the Physical Universe in order to bring all the vital elements of Nature into existence. Although, there are the Gods Who are part of the Spirits of the Spiritual Universe however, there is the One Who still endorses but indirectly controls all of the affairs of the Gods Who have hitherto been placed in charge of the Parallel Universes.

The Creator is entitled 'The LORD of the Spirits' or better still known as 'The Supreme GOD'. In my mother tongue, He is called "Mawu Ga" meaning "The Supreme GOD" or "The Great GOD".

Again, in my language He is known as "Mawu Sogbo Lisa" which means that, "The Supreme One Who is both Male and Female". In the Akan language He is known as "Onyankropong" which implies, "The Sovereign One".

The Ga people refer to Him as "Ataa Naa Nyugmo" which implies that, He is "The Great Father and Mother". Furniture, the Ga-Adangme natives call Him "Nyugmo Ofe" meaning, "The One Who is above all".

In the revelations of the Spirits of which my Eternal Mind or Self was enlightened to comprehend, I saw and knew that there is the Ultimate SPIRIT Who is the Supreme GOD over the Spirits; there are also, the Spirits Who are the

Gods and Goddesses of Nature;

There are the spirits who are angelic beings (such spirits are separated and classed into guarding and guiding angels as well as their being grouped into messengers like Gabriel and combattant arch-angels like Michael among others);

There are the spirits who are demonic beings; there are the spirits who are predestined and appointed by the LORD of the Spirits (thus the Supreme GOD) to be first of all incarnated as human beings called the Man on the terrestrial plane;

And secondly to be reincarnated again as human beings when they cannot complete their earthly mission or assignment before their demise;

And thirdly, men given the privilege to be transformed to appear on the Earth as having their previous but glorified human bodies with which they once used to be on the terrestrial plane when they could not fulfill their given assignments because they were exterminated;

And truncated owing to either the callousness of mankind as well as the carelessness of the same in respect of fatal road accidents, natural disasters, medical mistakes among others;

There are the Spirits Who are called the Aliens (such Spirits reside in the Spiritual Space yet come often into the terrestrial plane via flying saucers called the Unidentified Flying Objects or UFO's.

And these spirits are extremely audacious and dexterous in ultra-modern sophisticated technologies of which they several centuries in ancient times appeared on the planet Earth to stay awhile and to teach and instruct men on how to build sophisticated mansions and infrastructure and these left behind for mankind evidential proofs of their artistry which they did with various hardened rocks in places like India, Mexico, Africa but to mention only a few;

There are the spirits who are called the dwarfs and giants (such spirits are often connected to men and so have caused many individuals to vanish and who later returned with mysterious powers to help mankind in various avenues); there are the spirits of the dead called the ghosts (a number of such spirits dwell in the Spiritual World of Hades as those who have not fulfilled their missions or assignments are given either the privilege of being reincarnated or taught how to be transformed to appear on the terrestrial plane or the Earth);

There are the spirits which are called the animals both domestic and wildlife animals whether ferocious beasts or otherwise (such spirits are connected to men in respect of their respective, individual birthdays and destinies where some men have lions connected to them and others have tigers attached to them among others). For example, Jesus is attached to a lion hence, why He has been called to be 'the Lion of the Tribe of Yuda'. I am connected to Cancer or the Crab while my deceased dad was attached to Capricorn. The enumeration is quite longer than ever imagined.

All of these spirits are controlled yet they can work hand in hand with the LORD of the Spirits. The LORD of the Spirits is the Sustainer of the Universal Space and is the Universal Space Himself.

This is why He is the LORD of the Spirits. As the Universal Space is immeasurable and limitless so is the LORD of the Spirits.

The universal space and the LORD of the Spirits are one and the same. This is why there is no end to Divinity.

There is no end to Who and What GOD is to mankind. There is no end to the Being of GOD.

Let me say this to the renowned scientists. Scientists have hitherto tried to find out whether or not GOD exists and have not been able to see Him.

This is Who and What GOD is. GOD is the Physical Universe which has no end though its beginning is with GOD Himself.

GOD is the Spiritual Universe which is endless and measureless and which has neither a beginning nor an ending.

GOD is all that there is in Nature. GOD is the heaven of heavens. GOD is the waters, rivers, springs, fountains, seas and oceans. GOD is the angels and the spirits.

GOD is both the Light and the Darkness. GOD is both Spirit (John 4:24) and Man (Genesis 1:26). GOD is all things and everything. Finally GOD is anything in the universal space. In fact, He is all-in-one.

I advise those secular scientists to look nowhere else because GOD has been seen already by them.

Moses the prophet of YaHWeH described Him as being 'A Consuming Fire' (Deuteronomy 4:24). John the apostle of Jesus, the Christ described Him as being Light (1 John 1:5). He was both the Pillar of Fire by night and the Pillar of Clouds by day. He is both the Day and the Night.

It makes no sense to look for the LORD of the Spirits when HE can be found or seen in everything, anything and all things whether those ones which existed in the Past, or the ones that exist in the Present, or the ones that are yet to exist in the Future. He is the Past, Present and Future. He was Yesterday; He is Today and will be Tomorrow. Seeking Him further will be fruitless and irrelevant.

He is both here and there. He is now as well as then besides being forevermore. He is memorial and immemorial.

He is the beginning as well as the ending. Our obstinate refusal and ignorance in identifying ourselves as being both GOD or one of the Gods as well as being Man brings us down interminably. Our refusal to identify ourselves leads us to simply die like mere mortals.

We end up dying like mere men the moment we regard ourselves as being mortals only. GOD is both mortal and immortal. Man is mortal as well as immortal. In conclusion, GOD is as Good as He is evil for He knows both what is good and that which is evil.

GOD is extremely generous yet callous and tyrannical. GOD has been satisfied yet regrettable about His deeds.

I have truly identified myself as one of the Gods though as Man here on the Earth. In the revelation and understanding of our being Gods in the flesh, who rule, subdue and reign within the Physical Universe, we must place all circumstances under our feet no matter how huge they might be.

We are the Gods in the flesh hence, why we should not allow situations and circumstances overcome us to the point where we give up all hopes and are on the verge of dying.

We are well able to conquer and so we are invincible in every aspect of life experiences. This is the mystery of who we are and it has been hidden so that those who search for the unveiling of this mystery can become the Gods of all their circumstances.

This is all that this book seeks to reveal to you in many ways and to teach and instruct you thereby. It is my heartfelt premonition and prediction that by 2032, over a trillion copies of this book will have been sold and read by avalanche number of peoples globally. I have declared this and so shall it be in the Name of the LORD of the Spirits.

You are because I am alive for you and I am because you are alive for me. Whatever and whoever I am, you are also in respect of our original selves. Our original selves are a mystery to the world.

And the moment you and I are able to unveil that mystery, we shall become the Gods of this Physical Universe, whose determination and tenacity know no bounds in view of what problems are surrounding us. Whether they are circumstances or problems, we are the solution providers to all of the world's problems.

And no matter what happens, we are more than conquerors; for we are the Gods over every situation. The unveiling of our original selves leads us to become the Gods over every circumstance. You are the one who walks on high. We are those who walk on high therefore, we are 'Making It Now!' This is the mystery of your being and so this must be our experience together.

I am not expecting you to append an effective 'Amen' to this because, it is actually who you really were before time had begun and of what you are now for you are God in the flesh.

CHAPTER TWO

THE PURPOSE OF YOUR EXISTENCE

Dr Myles Munroe often said this:

"''Where the purpose of a thing is not known abuse is inevitable''"

Myles' statement on the fact that when the purpose of a thing usually everything in nature including man himself is not known man himself has the surest, inevitable tendency to abuse any of the minutest things existing in nature.

This is why his words are quite true and credible until today. It is the sole responsibility and duty of Man himself to find out the truest purpose of each and everything that exists in nature of which both great and small creatures as well as every little thing has been either put under his sovereignty or entrusted with him to have dominion over.

Elohim ordered Man to have dominion over the Physical Universe and to subdue everything which moves, lives and has its being in it. The dominion of Man transcends the governance and control over what we see as well as what is unseen.

Man rules over the affairs of the spiritual universe and that of the physical universe as well. The former universe is far larger and huger and vaster than the latter in several ways.

He, Man, has been honored to have and to be the co-authoritative being of the parallel universes. It is the invisible, supernatural forces that have permitted the existence of the things that we see in nature including those that we do not see to be under his control.

These supernatural forces are no other than the pre-existence of the Gods in coalition with the Supreme GOD, Who is the LORD of those Spirits. It is His sole responsibility to proffer purpose to every existing spirit.

The spirits who do not know their purposes are bound to appear disastrous, brutal and detrimental against the very existence of all the other spirits that dwell in the Spiritual Universe. Again, Myles confirmed that, "The greatest tragedy in life is not death, but a life without a purpose" hence, it is quite circumspect for each and every existing spirit to know its purpose as far as the Parallel Universes are concerned.

Avalanche spirits often get ensnared and entrapped when They forfeit the focal concentration of their respective, individual purpose hence, why they usually turn out to be disastrous and chaotic against the rest of the spirits.

A renowned Nigerian clergyman by the name of David Oyedepo who is both the founder and president of the Winners' Chapel globally once lamented, "A purposeless man is like a disaster going to occur somewhere" In fact, more often than seldom, various chaotic reactions and warring atmospheres in both the realms of the spiritual and that of the physical, become predominantly plentiful.

The spiritual universe has vastly spacious airways or pathways for the free movements of all the spirits. Individual purposes therefore, have direct connections with appointed times, seasons and periods and so whichever spirit that does not move in accordance with or comply with its purpose creates a stormy turbulence and topsy turvy for the rest wherever they might be at that moment hence, this in most cases results to brutal, combative show of powers between each other for instance, where such Spirits desire to come what may, prove their powers over or against one another simply because one has crossed the other's path.

It is highly difficult for certain spirits to lose their focus or purpose. Yet, there are only a few of some spirits that are liable to easily trespass or encroach on the routes of other spirits owing to their obstinacy and recalcitrance.

In fact, they are either careful or careless to cross the airways of others whether or not they are on their purposeful assignments. These spirits are usually the ones in whom witchcrafts dwell. They are therefore called witches and wizards.

Witches and wizards are not spirits rather, they are the human beings in whom the spirits and gifts called witchcrafts dwell.

It is possible to exterminate witches and wizards but extremely impossible to do so with their witchcrafts. This is because, what makes a witch or wizard powerful is no other thing than their witchcrafts.

Witchcrafts therefore are the spirits and gifts that are embedded in witches and wizards. It is therefore futile and practically nonsensical to fast and pray just to bring to death the Spirit which dwells in a witch or wizard.

It is quite easy to exterminate witches and wizards however, after they have been exterminated, their witchcrafts (spirits and gifts) wander around to seek and find the children of men to dwell in them.

I would like to reveal that of all the spirits in the universal space, it is those spirits of men that often fail to recollect their purposes while or during their existence on this terrestrial plane, thus the Earth.

When men assume the countenances of other spirits, they really become aware of their purposes as those Spirits.

For example, witchcraft is a spirit as well as a gift or talent hence, when men assume the purpose of witchcraft as witches, wizards and vampires they always know their purposes as such.

Of all the spirits, it is those spirits of men that are more powerful than all, except that they share equal powers and authority with GOD Himself.

This is because, the Supreme GOD Himself with the Gods themselves created and made the Man fearfully, wonderfully and specially before transferring them, thus the man and woman alike to the terrestrial plane (Earth).

Biblically, it is evident that when Elohim (thus the Supreme GOD and the Gods) created the Man, only HE (the Supreme GOD) breathed into His nostrils the breath of life and then Man became a living soul.

Elohim then entrusted complete and full dominion into the care of the Man. Elohim ordered Him to have dominion in order to subdue the Earth and to dominate every living thing which exists on it. This is why no other spirits can have the right or freedom to invade the terrestrial plane without the sole permission of the Man.

> "*The ancient, Israelite king, David who was both a psalmist and prophet once stated, "I am fearfully and wonderfully made". Man was not created in the image and likeness of GOD. Rather, He the Man was created (thus was made) the image and likeness of GOD Himself.*"

This makes Man no different from GOD for He the Man, is one of the Gods Himself. Nothing more or less than being the very image and likeness of GOD Himself. Man is simply and directly GOD Himself. In fact, Man and GOD are one and the same in several ways.

This is why Man is more powerful than the Spirits that are the Angelic Beings yet he is liable to become less powerful than these angels when he falls through in his original or truest identity as GOD Himself in his existence on the terrestrial plane.

Man is more powerful than all the Spirits Who are Demonic Beings yet becomes less audacious when he fails to identify with Himself that He is actually GOD Himself. Man is not just a representative of GOD but is fully GOD yet He is full of Flesh and Blood.

There is nowhere in the Bible where any other Spirits are described or said to have Blood in Them besides Man and the Supreme GOD. In fact, in the Book of Acts precisely the twentieth chapter and in the twenty-eighth verse, Saint Lucas a medical practitioner and who was a good friend of the apostle Paul once wrote:

"Take heed therefore unto yourselves, and to all the flock, over the which the Holy Ghost hath made you overseers, to feed the church of GOD, which He (GOD) hath purchased with His (GOD's) own Blood"

By this therefore, I can boldly and confidently confirm what my Spirit received with regards to the above-stated biblical verse that only the spirits of both Man and the Supreme GOD Himself are said to have blood existing in them.

This is quite incredible yet believably, it is stated in black and white in the Bible. Angelic Beings do not possess blood in their systems except when they transform (convert or change) themselves into human beings.

The privilege to be incarnated or reincarnated has not been given to Angelic Beings by the LORD of the Spirits. The privileges of both incarnation and reincarnation have been given to only Man and the Supreme GOD Himself.

I would expatiate further on this somewhere in this book. I want to reveal that in order for those two hundred premeditating and rebellious angels Who were led by Samyaza to come to the Earth with the common purpose to choose the beautiful daughters of men for marriage and to teach and instruct the children of men on various technological artistry and innovations, they had to transform themselves into human beings before they could achieve their united purpose.

When these transformers (defiant angels) were able to achieve their common purpose, They had sexual intercourse with the daughters of men whom they had married and they bore children with them.

Their children were those giants of ancient times who had caused a huge cosmological havoc to the Earth by mishandling and maltreating the sons of men because they had lost their purpose. They became a disaster to humanity and mankind.

There is a partial evidence of their existence in the sixth chapter of the Book of Genesis written by Moses. In order for you to understand the following verses better, I have applied some addendums for some amount of comprehension. These addendums further amplify the original and true meaning of these verses as revealed in the Bible. Please read and study the following verses carefully.

Genesis 6:1-4

> “*"And it came to pass (thus in ancient times), when men began to multiply on the face of the earth (the terrestrial plane), and daughters were born unto them (simply men),*
>
> *‘That the sons of God (thus Angelic Beings or ’Ben Ha Elohim‘ which should have been translated as "the Sons of the Gods" of which All of Them are under the Supreme GOD Who is the LORD of the Spirits) saw the daughters of men that they were fair (beautiful and seductive in their countenances and appearances); and they (angelic beings) took them wives (angelic beings transformed themselves into human beings in order to marry the daughters of men) of all which they (angelic beings) chose’.*
>
> *‘And the LORD said, My Spirit (for GOD is Spirit Himself) shall not always strive with Man, for that He also is flesh (this reveals that Man shares the same original being with the Supreme GOD; it furthermore reveals that GOD will come into the terrestrial plane someday to take on flesh and blood or is flesh Himself because of the use of the words ’for He the Man is also flesh‘ by GOD Himself): yet His (Man’s) days shall be an hundred and twenty years (six scores).*
>
> *’There were giants (the children which the daughters of men bore for those angelic beings in*

> *view of marriage) in the earth in those days (ancient times); and also after that, when the sons of GOD (angelic beings) came in unto the daughters of men, and they bare children to them, the same became mighty men which were of old, men of renown"*"

It is a fatal tragedy for one to lose their original identity and purpose. When people's purposes are misplaced and lost, it appears that they become disastrous, catastrophic and dangerous to the society, the community, the world and the whole physical universe at large.

Earlier on somewhere in this book, I unveiled just a glimpse of how angelic beings have not been given the privilege to be incarnated and reincarnated. The privileges of both incarnation and reincarnation have been left for solely the spirits of men and that of GOD Himself.

The spirits of both angels and demons do not share in the privileges of incarnation and reincarnation with GOD and Man, except that they share in the privilege of transformation, which is the third secret and invisible doorway to the terrestrial plane.

Both Man and GOD have the powers to be incarnated, reincarnated and transformed in order to enter into the Earth.This is why Man is God and that Man's original being is that He is God Himself.

Biblically, it is revealed that Jesus Christ existed with GOD hence why nothing in the Parallel Universes was created or made without Him. Christ Jesus according to the Gospel of John the beloved, was in the beginning with GOD hence, He shared in the existence of all of creation. John's Gospel has this revelation in **John 1:1-3:**

"In the beginning was the Word, and the Word was with GOD, and the Word was GOD'
'The same was in the beginning with GOD'
'All things were made by Him; and without Him was not any thing made that was made"

These verses of the Bible have gone a long way to prove the Divinity of the Man, Jesus. He was originally Christ, the Spirit Who shared in the existence of creation with the Supreme GOD, Who is His Father (the Eternal Source).

The LORD of the Spirits is the Supreme GOD, while Christ was one of those Spirits Who caused the existence of the Parallel Universes. Christ had pre-existed before He was born of a virgin called Mary, whom had been chosen by the LORD of the Spirits to be the favored woman among women.

Christ as being a Spirit came through the secret, natural doorway of incarnation in respect of this chosen handmaiden of the Supreme GOD. And when the appointed period of time was fully complete, Mary put to bed an innocent baby full of smiles whose name was Jesus the CHRIST (the Anointed One).

By this therefore, the unique body of the Savior of Israel was called JESUS. He argued and debated with the scribes and the Pharisees that although He was not yet fifty years old, He had been in existence before Abraham, that rich but humble, ancient patriarch who became the pioneering father of the Jews and the Hebrew Language altogether.

As Man, He was JESUS of Nazareth that Man of Galilee but as a Spirit Being He was CHRIST the Son of GOD Himself. In Jesus the CHRIST, dwells the Efficacious Blood of the LORD of the Spirits. And this is simply how both Man and GOD are the only Beings that have Precious Blood flowing in Their Veins.

Angelic beings do not possess blood in their systems. Demonic beings do not possess blood in their veins. Animals do have blood flowing in them yet they do not share in the existence of creation. Man controls and tames ferocious animals bringing them under control by his dominion.

Just as all animals whether they are physical or spiritual, ferocious or otherwise are supposed to serve Man when he realizes his dominion over them. Angels are also created to serve Man. Demons can be controlled by Man because He has been given all the powers to subject them to his dominion and authority. I used an important verse of Scripture earlier on and so would therefore like to remind you of it by reiteration.

"Take heed therefore unto yourselves, and to all the flock, over the which the Holy Ghost hath made you overseers, to feed the church of GOD, which He (GOD) hath purchased with His (GOD's) own blood"

This verse has further solidified and confirmed that though we have accepted the truth that the Supreme GOD is SPIRIT, has blood flowing in His veins.

> "*In Genesis chapter six the Supreme GOD had pointed out this truth, "...for He (Man) is also flesh" The revelation here is clear that GOD possesses flesh and blood in His veins besides being 'A Spirit'. It is therefore, only GOD and Man Who share flesh and blood as well as their being 'spirit beings'. Of course, both the Supreme GOD and Man are the only beings who share humanity and divinity together. This makes Man the 'image and likeness' of the Supreme Deity.*"

There is therefore, now no denying of this original truth. This has been what Jesus the CHRIST came to both reveal and prove about His original being with the Supreme GOD to all of mankind and being truthfully a part of humanity when He came and walked the shores of sea while on this terrestrial plane. This revelation should let Man recognize that He was pre-existent before the existence of creation.

Man is therefore, Human as well as Divine. Jesus was and still is Human and Divine. GOD is Himself both Divine and Human. Man is first of all Human as long as He lives here yet Divine. Jesus proved to the Pharisees of His day that He was Human yet Divine. In conclusion, the LORD of the Spirits is as Divine as HE is Human.

I am God and so therefore, I am the Son of the Most High GOD. Whatever and whoever GOD is, I am here on the Earth, and so nothing can hinder my dominion with which I rule, reign and subdue the Earth. This what makes me mysterious for it is my experience.

This was revealed to Saint John the Beloved. I have amplified it for your reference in respect of myself as a Man who is also, God. The addendums are there for clarity and comprehension.

1 John 4:15

> ***“"Whosoever shall confess that Jesus is the Son of GOD, GOD dwelleth in Him, and He in GOD’.***
>
> ***‘And I (as Man) have known and believed the love that GOD hath to Me (as Man). GOD is Love; and He that dwelleth in Love dwelleth in GOD, and GOD in Him’.***
>
> ***‘Herein is My Love made perfect, that I may have boldness in the day of judgment: because as He (GOD) is, so am I (as Man) in this world***

(the physical universe and the terrestrial plane altogether)."”

This is why I can boldly and confidently declare that:

> ***“I am unshakable, I am unmovable, I am ubiquitous, I am powerful, I am authoritative, I am an unconquerable conqueror, I am invincible, I am invisible, I am universal, I am supreme, I Am God, I am human, I am divine and finally I am Man. This is not just a bold confession of who I want to be but, a declaration of 'Who I Am' here on the Earth.”***

I am Hyperion and so therefore, I am 'Making It Now! You are Hyperion and so therefore, You are 'Making It Now' in view of the mystery of your original self and this should be your personal lot

“LITTLE DROPS OF WATER MAKE THOUSAND LITERS”

While I was growing up in one of the most impoverished suburbs of the Greater Accra Region in my country, I learnt a number of activities such as fishing, farming, footballing, gold smithing the list is not longer than one can ever imagine.

Anyways, I hail from Atsiavi, an ancient town located around the Ketu South District in the Volta Region of the Republic of Ghana. Of course, Ghana is directly situated in the West African vicinity of the African Continent.

What caught my rapt attention was (and still is) farming and this ancient, traditional activity ranked the number one on my personal list during my childhood years.

Biblically, the very first ancient profession that Elohim entrusted into the care of the very first man created by Them was farming as we have read many times in the Bible. Agriculture as well as farming is either animal husbandry or crop farming or otherwise in a large perspective.

Adam was commanded by Elohim to till the land and to take care of the garden of Eden. When his children Cain and Abel were of age, the Bible emphatically states that the former Cain, chose to do his father's profession thus crop farming, while the latter Abel, trained himself on animal husbandry (Genesis 2:15; 4:2-4).

This makes farming the number one activity or profession on my list as stated earlier. I would like to state that I had closely observed gradually that a good but prudent farmer would not sow seeds in just any soil. He had a simple list of particular soils which are practically conducive for the sowing of seeds and which would allow for germination and growth.

Hereafter, a gradual growth took place and where nature would systematically or eventually lead the plants to the farmer's reaping of a bountiful harvest afterwards.

In fact, a whole lot of vital, agricultural statistics of processes went on before the great harvest of cash crops for instance, would take place. However, I would like to save us all those significant, farming processes, which are basically and usually done through the sole responsibility of the farmer per se.

To this in effect, I say profoundly that being in the right and most appropriate environment really matters and so therefore, it is quite vital to do all that it takes within one's power and ability to be found in the most appropriate environ.

A wise farmer would eschew planting among rocky areas, and the following would not be any of his choices of soils. Thus, neither the course sand nor the clayey soil is his required choice or better still, his best selection. I could mention a number of other bad soils but the list might be a bit tall here, so to mention only a few of them is quite acceptable.

Most definitely sometimes, the farmer would choose both plantable and required soil say, black soil to do the sowing of the seeds. This often made the farmer appear as a discreet individual amidst other farmers, who are at least as good as he is.

This goes a long way to prove the farmer's professionalism irrespective of what that farmer's gender is as well as his being an experienced farmer who has studied most of the natural tendencies and properties of all the available soils roundabout him.

The farmer surely knows and has an enumeration of bad soils and those of good soils as well, nevertheless, he really decides to choose the most plantable soils for quite a number of some particular seeds.

Please, permit me to lead you via an acceptable diversion here. I would like to state that sowing of seeds generally cannot be likened to the saving of money in the bank or any of the credit unions in my country.

In my opinion, sowing of seeds or emphatically farming can be compared to a massive investment with or at the bank.

> *"In most cases, I would say that saving money is viewed in respect of the apostle Paul's words as we often read in* ***Galatians 6:7:*** *"...For what a man sows, is also what he reaps". I want to use Paul's*

words in the sense that if one saved up to US$1,000.00 thus, one thousand dollars, he actually would withdraw simply one thousand dollars. If he left US$1,000.00 with any of the numerous banks whose interest rate is 15% per annum, then this person would withdraw US$1,150.00 (Eleven Hundred and Fifty Dollars) after at least a year."

The interest rate upon this said amount of money from his bank might just be petty, minute and meagre. In the case of an investment, one cannot invest thousand dollars (US$1,000.00), in order to withdraw just thousand dollars (US$1,000.00), a few weeks afterwards.

This does not happen in most cases because, one actually, withdraws more, hence, why many individuals go in for investments. Investment simply, allows you to free your thousand dollars to work for you instead of making it lie motionless in the bank like savings do in the varied accounts of many a people in my country.

The results in an investment after several months, are hugely impressive, and to describe it as gigantic, is not an understatement at all. Experientially, I have learnt (and I am still learning, anyways) over the years, that with or without any educational documents (I do refer to certificates and awards) and backgrounds, a large number of individuals no matter their provenances and personalities, can make it.

But at large and however, it depends on the kind of environment in which they find themselves oftentimes. Every environment is your soil, and a good one of course, just like the plantable soil of a farmer's. In essence, if your environment was bad enough, then, consider the fact that, you would struggle in it.

And if your environment is good, you will eventually, prevail successfully in it. Sometimes, one might fall a prey to the old Latin wise words, ***"Aluta continua!"*** which in the English language means, ***"The struggle continues!"***. The point is, why should the struggle continue for you?

This is so because, you have chosen the wrong pathways and environment to make it but, you would struggle enough to do so at all cost. This is experientially evident in various parts of the African continent for myriads of Africans.

In the same vein, if your environment was a good one, you would boom and strive easily and within a number of months you would be catapulted to the zenith of riches.

This is possible to happen in the shortest possible period if one had the best of environments where he or she grew up. In Africa a young boy struggles to fend for himself because, the environment has been heightened with a number of corrupt deals and deeds.

The system of administration has made it more difficult to pull through and practically there is the availability of corrupt leadership with a bunch of corrupt leaders lurking in nooks and crannies of the African Continent.

If corrupt leaders with their corrupt leadership oversee the administrative affairs of the government in power everything goes higgledy piggledy in its everyday economy.

In essence and naturally, the environment of Africa appears and seems lucrative, and the researched facts are existent, owing to its vast array of rich, natural resources such as uranium, diamond, gold, bauxite, magnesium and what have you.

We cannot be oblivious of this reality, however, that each of the 54 countries of Africa appears poorer than we can all ever imagine.

My own country Ghana, for instance, many of her people always boasted of and still do boast of the rich mineral reserve which she has yet, it always hitherto appears that she is poor to the core simply because, she has had for several years a consecutive number of political governments which come into power or government and did vacate her governing body as richer men and affluent politicians and who were originally not rich but partially poor.

However, in all of these recounted above, the country is left to remain poor hitherto. To this essence, it would be quite impossible to sleep in oblivion in respect of what Africa possesses as we all see the continent appear in reality.

Africa boasts of avalanche, natural resources that are capable of making the continent a celestial palace here on earth, yet, it has turned out to be a terrestrial hell to all and sundry living in it. If a man went round at least some prominent parts of the continent of Africa, and in whichever country of it which he might find himself and if he peradventure, saw any millionaire somewhere in Africa, that man possibly a foreigner, should salute with a "military honor" that African millionaire whom he had come across and to bestow upon this African millionaire many an accolade would not be a bad idea at all.

African millionaires and billionaires should and must be celebrated annually throughout the African terrain. I would prefer to use a relative scenario here which often exists in the advance foreign or European terrain, and thus, where a boy who grows up in countries like Canada, Britain, Holland, in any parts of Europe and elsewhere in the continent of Australia, ends up comprehending the meaning of "Little drops of water, make thousand litres".

Somehow, this boy is bound to strive in such good environments with all his great ideas because, each of the above-mentioned countries has the appropriate tendencies of transforming this particular boy into becoming a multi-millionaire or perhaps, a billionaire come what may. African youths always discuss other youths of their age, and I mean those youths who live in other countries especially the advanced and developed ones. In many cases, several youths of the United States, Canada, Germany, Australia, Sweden and more are the favorite ones in their constant discussions, all the day long.

Practically and literally they have all the time at their disposal to talk about those youths for many decades until they bite the dust. If for instance, an Austrian girl had all the basic needs of life such as food, clothing and shelter for a good start and probably did not even attend any of the best of schools in her country, she would end up in most cases as a rich woman in comparison to an African lass.

In this current dispensation of our generation, almost all the African youths owe a lot of indebtedness to the advent of sophisticated technologies globally.

Many a technology has helped to a high level, lots of the youths worldwide, especially, those youths in the parts of our African world, to become millionaires. The system is such that whatever anybody does somehow or anyhow, has the likelihood of trending viral and this practically, converts to lots of money for them.

The legally registered activities, whether they are videos or something else, multiplies into their being rich and famous anywhere they might be in the globe. I would like us to accept unanimously, 360 days for a year and where there are twelve months in a year, we should agree to make each month, just thirty days.

And this is what I wish to say here. I cannot be sure if this story was true or not but, I was told this story by one of my deceased uncles, Danny. Uncle Dan narrated that there was once this boy who resided in Accra. In fact, he told me this story when I was younger that this Ghanaian boy, who was six years old in those days had begun saving at least £1.00 each day and by his consistency he was able to save in a wooden box some money for himself a whole year.

Be reminded that we had earlier on agreed to take three hundred and sixty days for a year. In respect of this, the boy saved £360.00 that particular year. He agreed with himself to persist in savings and which he continued gradually for the next decade.

On his seventeenth birthday, he had saved three thousand, nine hundred, sixty pounds sterling in those days. Times were very favorable and considerate towards people in those days, so then £3,960.00 was a whole lot of money for them. Even today, three thousand, nine hundred, sixty pounds sterling is equivalent to GHS32,052.39 (Thirty-two thousand, fifty-two and thirty-nine pesewas) or more over time.

Most of the Ghanaian citizens accept the old order of parlance calling the above-mentioned amount of money, three hundred and twenty million, five hundred and twenty-three thousand, nine hundred old cedis and zero pesewa (¢320,523,900.00).

The reality is that, the Ghanaian lad in my narration could be a millionaire at least, today. Practically, the current trend of technology with respect to the social media platforms can easily make even small children who know the way out in the midst of technology to become multi-millionaires.

The fact is that, it has not only made white children rich but, black children have had their fair share of the cake of technology through social interactions and platforms.

I have had a train of thoughts for at least half a decade and have accrued just one important observation in that regard and this would astonish you thoroughly, as I persist in this book. I observed that the worst environment which is capable of obstructing and hindering any young man to prospering financially, is but his negative mentality or ideas.

Any young man who prides himself in a negative mindset is bound to find himself in a bad soil like a seed or better still, any seed, and no matter how many times that he plants himself in the soil of negative thoughts and ideas, he cannot prosper financially and moving forward would be a hard nut to crack for him.

This is why most of our young folks parade and visit with a number of powerful shrines and idols so that the fetish custodians of such shrines and idols would help them with what is called 'blood-money'. Many exchange their lives with something else but diabolical, in respect of blood-money and until they go through a number of diabolical rituals, they can never become rich and wealthy.

A few of the African youths have diligently struggled to become rich and wealthy yet, many others see and describe them as *"Sakawa Boys"* who had gone in for blood-money. The word 'sakawa' is often used in the Ghanaian local parlance of my country, as a term for the boys, guys and men, who are practically involved in and deal in 'blood-cash' and the point is that no one ever knew of how they became rich all of a sudden.

In Nigeria, *"Sakawa Boys"* are called *"Yahoo Boys"* because they are involved in rituals and sacrifices of blood. They often use charms to collect money from their online business partners and rich friends. Some of them really, might have been affluent through good, hardworking means yet, they are termed 'sika duro guys' in other words, 'medicine money' which is literally blood money. Quite a number of these youths are members of some sort of occultic groups as well as other demonic sects.

There are various avenues that are conducive for the making of money and which are at least the right ways, yet a larger amount of the African youths indulge in performing bloody rituals in order to become wealthy. Those who engage in bribery and corruption are just countable while the ones who are into illegal and contraband goods are but a few.

For a number of decades now, myriads of the African youths have had negative thoughts and mentality, and to be frank, I see a merely, obvious reason for their becoming financially poor. They cannot prosper financially, amidst negative mindset and evil thoughts, and even if around them, was the lucid existence of wealth, they would be so poor financially.

They are extremely impoverished in such a way that they can never be of any good use to their communities or societies, and to this existence, one of the ancient kings of Israel, King Solomon, once said in the twenty-third chapter of Proverbs of the seventh verse that:

“***"For as he thinketh in his heart, so is he..."***”

Let me drive my wheel towards the route of clarity here. if I had thought that I would not make it in life no matter how hard I tried, I would have been poor in several ways and forms: mentally, spiritually and physically.

A bunch of negative-thought-driven youths may have all the rich, natural resources at their disposal yet, they will become the proud members of poverty. Poverty will be their portion always, the kind of youths who harbour negativity and enrich bad ideas.

There are a quantity of young men who are practically poor, yet, they are very rich because they flaunt positive thoughts in their premises. As they continue to feed their minds with positive thoughts, they are bound to become affluent financially, owing to the positive thoughts and ideas that they possess. In fact, it is just a matter of time and chance, they will appear as their thoughts and ideas are.

I have had the privilege of following critically after those youths whose thoughts were bad from the start and the massive pessimistic results that came to appear as regards those bad or negative thoughts of theirs.

Most of such young individuals languished in jails as inmates to hardened criminals like murderous armed robbers, kidnappers and child traffickers; and the least of them is not encouraging to posterity, so I would end here. The youths who patronized positive thoughts in their past were those ones who are seen in our various societies to be the enjoyers of good life today.

The outcomes of positive thoughts are highly profitable and life-changing to all and sundry. A positive thinking youth is one who is always optimistic in all circumstances, and the same is quite hopeful in making it come what may. This youth is the one who becomes a role model to others whether they are his peers or older than he is.

A positive thinking individual is not opportunistic at the expense of others. Being opportunistic at the expense of others makes one a gold digger. A negative thinking person is one who is opportunistic at the expense of others, in the sense that he uses criminal schemes, tricks and techniques to rob others of their properties and monies.

Again, a negative thinking person is one who improvises criminal schemes just to extort money from people. This negative thinking youth or person is opportunistic, hence, the future is not bright on his side. A positive thinking individual is opportunistic at the opportunities that are available to everyone; he becomes smart enough to grab the best of opportunities at his disposal so that he can set the pace for others to follow.

There are a handful of billionaires in the world today, who are rich and famous currently by being opportunistic at grabbing opportunities amongst their fellowmen and such rich men and women are Aliko Dangote of Nigeria, Bill Gates of the United States of America, His Highness Sheikh Khalifa bin Zayed Al Nahyan (deceased former President of the United Arab Emirates), the Crown Prince Hamdan bin Mohammed bin Rashid al Makhtoum of Dubai, Oprah Winfrey, Beyoncé Knowles amongst others and these were all opportunistic in respect of grabbing the best of the billion opportunities in their worlds.

Many of our political parties have leaders who do not think that Africa has the appropriate capacity to make it like the advanced and developed countries, hence, why amidst the vast array of rich, natural resources, Africans do hitherto, languish in abject poverty. I wish I would say that rather, it is Africans who are poor than Africa being poor. The continent of Africa is a multi-billionaire among the other continents of the whole, wide world. In the midst of all these mineral resources, its inhabitants and dwellers are obviously and pathetically impoverished.

Our leaders are highly poor mentally, hence, in the sedentary of wealth and rich minerals, they relocate their respective, individual countries in the lands of poverty. The worst of all of these, is how they push many a multitude of people, who are African youths into poverty and make it extremely difficult for their youths to thrive financially.

In fact, they make the economic ambience of commercialization, quite an impossible and unbearable one for the youths especially. African youths encounter a list of hard times in such a way that it makes their sailing ships find it difficult to sail through the storms and turbulence of the high seas and oceans.

To all of these, it is a high time that African youths wherever they might be, and in fact, the positive-thinking ones, said that enough is enough to all the breakdowns brought to them by our corrupt leaders with their corrupt leadership, and allowed the freedom and justice of our hearts and unity, bring to them the times of breakthroughs.

It is just about time that the African youths and even our children began saying, we are 'Making It Now!' no matter what. They must defy all odds to boldly declare over the hills and valleys that we are indeed, 'Making It Now!' Yes, 'We Can!' and we are 'Making It Now!'

And 'Making It Now! is the best decision that any individual can make in order to become either a millionaire or billionaire today in any parts of the globe. So therefore, it becomes helpful to admonish all the young people wherever they might be in the parts of the globe to always, work diligently, on being some unique individuals, and not on having material things, for with whom they become, they will have all that they need.

It is a high time everyone awakened to the reality that we see in view of sophisticated technologies globally.

Many a problem will try to play pranks on you but be steadfast and determined that you are a solution to that problem. When evil tries to engulf you with several temptations in order to overcome you, just be rest assured that you are a good God over it, then it will be placed under your footstool by your dominion.

> "*You are Hyperion and so therefore, you are conquering all the diabolical energies that are surrounding you.*
>
> *I am the one who walks on high with the Creator of the Universes and this makes me Hyperion and so therefore, I am 'Making It Now!'*"

CHAPTER THREE

A COB OF CORN IS WORTH SEVERAL MAIZE

"A Cob Of Corn Is Worth Several Maize"

Many people for several decades have not for once given any attention and regard to a cob of corn. They have neither considered a single seed of pepper nor have thought of sowing a seed of orange.

To many folks, it does not constitute anything expedient and it does not amount to anything of value, so many men have ignored it; and this, I am referring to any seed of any crop such as pepper, tomato, okra, aubergine, garden eggs and many more.

Sometimes, even farmers have ignored a single seed because most of them have believed that in planting the seed of any crop at all, a farmer should sow them in threes and fours. Having undergone several hardships in the past, I have for many years through some amount of experience given value and worth to single seeds.

I had in the past enjoyed aubergines in my meals, yet, it all started with my sowing them from just a single seed. To be honest with you, I got just a single seed of the aubergine and sowed it; however, after sometime, I reaped a handful of aubergines during harvest.

From there, I prepared a meal with just a number of them and left one aubergine crop. I left it somewhere to dry up and then in the course of time, I opened it up to acquire the seeds in it in order to sow them.

For your information, I had a few seeds from that particular aubergine which had been kept somewhere by me overtime. I sowed all the seeds and with time as required, the earth gave me a bountiful harvest, and I mean this relatively.

My experience in farming for at least two decades has been that of subsistent farming. I did farming just to cater for my personal feeding. Most farmers follow seasons and times with respect to farming for many years and I had followed such pattern of farming on the credit of subsistent farming. This practical activity has helped me for many years as I had been fed well from it.

In Ghana, almost every farmer likes to plant and harvest maize, since it constitutes most of the local meals of the individual ethnic people. Many local dishes or meals are prepared with maize, and so the maize crop helps the Ghanaian individual family to a large extent.

I had sowed cobs of corn for at least some years hence, why I have come to give an extreme regard to a cob of corn. This is what gave me the wise statement as you read a while ago, as the superscription and this I mean: A cob of corn is worth thousand maizes.

This principal statement has really been of a colossal assistance to me in many ways. I have already told you that

I have practised subsistent farming for at least two decades; and which implies that I have not done farming on a large scale before. I did a large scale farming once and that was some years ago, in 2010.

I simply had committed myself to subsistent farming to feed myself for years. Large scale farming requires a lot of efforts and it is quite stressful and financially, demanding. For instance, one needs to acquire a large parcel of land for a large scale farming. Another instance is that one needs to do a lot of weeding and a number of other activities, and this what makes it stressful.

I really do not have the natural strength to be committed to a large scale farming and so I fear to venture into it. Several years ago, when I tried to go into a large scale farming, it had been a friend of mine who convinced me to go into cassava farming specifically on a large scale and in this, I spent an amount of money which is equivalent to US$100.00 to lease just a half of an acre of land for two years.

Moreso, I had to spend like US$50.00 to purchase some cassava sticks, with the conveying cost to the place of the farmland excluded. Again, I had to bring in farm hirelings to help me in planting all the cassava sticks.

My hirelings and I managed to put into the earth 5,000 cassava sticks and the expenditure amounted to US$120.00, being shared among my four hirelings. And when weeds started growing among the germinated cassava plants, I had to spend some US$100.00 to get some hirelings to clear off the weeds amidst the cassava plants.

This process went on every three months until the cassava plants were ready for harvest. The entire process and procedure took me a year and half, in other words, 18 months to reap a bountiful harvest, and which became the very first time in my life to reap on a large scale, after over twenty years of subsistent farming and this was done all in the name of diverting at least once into a large scale farming through the advice of my good friend Louis.

Anyways, I had to feed my family on the harvested cassava plants and I sold some and afterwards, the sum of money I accrued from the sales helped to cater for a number of personal needs and to buy some basic needs for the family.

In a nutshell, I spent an amount of money totalling US$550.00 and be honest with myself, I did not get this money at once. It took me sometime to get it and in fact, money came in bits and pieces. The fact is, whenever, I got some cash, I used it to accomplish some necessary arrangements on the cassava farm.

The above-mentioned amount of money went into covering for the payment of leasing of a parcel of land, the hiring of tractor to clear of the weeds on the land, the payment given to the farm hirelings to plant the cassava sticks, the intermittent clearing of weeds quarterly, and a handful of other needful things but to state only a few.

I would like everyone reading this book to know that many a Ghanaian citizen, struggled extremely, in order to achieve certain little things for themselves and I have been personally, cheerful with those things that I struggled to acquire. I dropped out of school when I was in the Senior Secondary in 1998, upon failing woefully, the Senior Secondary School Certificate Examinations (WAEC-SSSCE).

And in those days, times were hard for me, although, several other people passed through similar ordeals. I would by a flimsy excuse trace this to the loss of parental control rather than the lack of it.

In fact, all of these occurred because, my biological parents were separated in 1987 but were divorced in 1993, without the signing of any papers of divorcement at the court. They did this on the accord of individuality. My father and mother had been legally married in 1970 and sources said that their marriage was a gloriously, grand wedding in those days. I was once told by someone, a relative, that my parents were the first couple to have been wedded in their church in those years.

I never bothered to ask any of my parents where their holy matrimony took place. I did not get the opportunity to re-sit my examinations in 1999 until 2001, when I had visited with my elder sister, Precious Abigail, who has been married to Alexander Thompson. My elder sister then advised me to attend some remedial classes but, I refused.

I did refuse because, I was then being blindfolded by the active zeal for Christianity to become a renowned clergyman. However, I made a personal decision to self-educate myself and to be trained in the Manna Bible Institute, which is still located in a province of Accra called Teshie.

I read several books and always took to learning in various libraries whether they be private or public. I graduated as the Best Bible Scholar and Valedictorian in 2003 when I was at Manna Bible Institute.

I had begun writing poems, informative articles and tributes while I was there though this had started when I was younger in age. Many colleagues who had read my informative articles, poems or tributes lauded me for my dexterity in writing such pieces of information.

Some family members who had read them were amazed and appreciated me for my efforts. Many of my classmates, schoolmates and course mates who are alive today can clearly attest to this fact.

A number of my relatives who can testify to this fact are deceased yet there remains a few who can simply confirm this fact. The last of the few great individuals who had encouraged me over the years died somewhere in January of the year, 2022 and he bit the dust at the age of 87.

He was called Emmanuel Bernard Amebley, a man who had worked and served the nation of Ghana and also has worked for a number of the great statesmen in my country. A decade after my refusal to re-sit my examinations, I have hitherto lived with a number of regrets yet I still am glad that I did not refuse to self-educate myself until now.

There is a huge difference between schooling and education. The former is limited to the confinement of a school building where teachers teach a student to know how to work with the pieces of information in respect of a curricula, while education is not limited to anything, but allows a student to learn both within the box as well as without it.

Education helps a student to learn irrespective of their age. It is actually, education which helped many of the prominent worldly statesmen to become great statesmen for their renowned countries.

I would like to make a mention of the sixteenth President of the United States of America, by the name of Abraham Lincoln, that all the schooling which he had was not more than a year, however, by education, he spent time to read the Bible many times, and took the pains to walk many a mile to collect or borrow books in order to become a good lawyer.

He was determined though, but all of this is connected to self-education. I know quite a countable number of friends, who felt that after being schooled, all they could do is but to work and work for money. To me it was a different opinion, because, I saw it as an opportunity to educate myself after having dropped out of school.

The schooling which continues and persists after being out of the confinement of the four walls of a school building with teachers in it, is nothing else apart from being called education. One of Ghana's Boxing legends did not attend school, howbeit, he realized the necessity for being educated and so he learnt in order to command at least some good English language to this day and he is no other man than our own Professor Barima Azumah Nelson (Zoom Zoom) who chalked many successes in the area of Sports in view of Boxing.

There are many Americans who never had the chance to attend schools yet saw it fit to be educated and today, many youths take them as their role models. Education is therefore, one that should be more accepted than being schooled in the four walls of a school building. I have a lot to say here but to mention only a few.

I want to state that, the pragmatic benefits of maize to many a Ghanaian household, should cause the individual members domiciled in it to have a sure reason for being grateful to one of the several feminine deities called Asaase Yaa, in the Akan language. The Akans constitute the largest population and they possess the largest ethnic groups of people in all of Ghana, and these Akans for instance are the Ashantis, Fantis, Akuapems and more.

In the lingua franca of the Queen of England and other states, this significant spirit, Asaase Yaa, is the so-called Mother Earth. 'Asaase' in the Akan language means 'earth' or 'land' in the English language, while 'Yaa' is the name often christened to any female child, that is born on Thursday, precisely.

Most of the Ghanaian traditional ancestries have had a relationship with the polytheistic system of worship and beliefs. This was also the case of the Hebrews or Jews when the name "Elohim" comes to mind. It is a polytheistic word rather than it is monotheistic. This has been passed on to their posterity or descendants in several forms.

Every true and genuine son of the soil belongs to an ancestry which made him believe in the real existence of deities and thus, I mean polytheism. This was our practical belief system prior to the visit of the white man with Christianity to the land of Africa, thus, the black man, and precisely here, I am referring to the Gold Coast, now Ghana.

The advent of Christianity in most parts of Africa pushed many of the indigenous people to waive their polytheistic system of worship of the Gods to a monotheistic form of worship of the God of the Bible or better still the special deity of the Europeans.

In reference to the past, I would not mince words to affirm that Asaase Yaa is extremely connected to great abundance, active fertility and bountiful harvest. This special feminine deity is not the only feminine deity being worshipped by us and with this I mean, she is not the only feminine deity that is worshipped by many Ghanaians, and perhaps, most Africans also worship her, but have an indigenous name for her.

Traditionally, most farmers always ascribe a heartfelt obeisance to this feminine deity and hence why such traditional farmers often pour libations in honour of her before the farming seasons commenced. Traditional farmers believe that this particular feminine deity is the one responsible for the provision of great abundance of harvest in several folds to them.

This is why in almost every indigenous part of the Ghanaian environment, farmers are not permitted to attend to their farmlands on specific days. It is a taboo to attend to your farmland on a specifically, unique day of restrictions.

Breaching this custom or tradition is tantamount to a capital punishment or banishment from the land. In the village where I once owned a cassava farmland, farmers are not allowed to attend to their farms on Tuesdays and Thursdays.

The reason being that Tuesdays are meant to be used to cleanse the lands in respect of the farms, while Thursdays are used for the honour of the feminine deity called Asaase Yaa. It is said that some encounters of farmers had met with this feminine deity face to face and the rest of the story was a bad omen upon the families of those disobedient farmers.

By this In my view with respect to my several years of experience of life, I had felt and believed that Elohim (the Gods) created the universe in such a way that the earth in particular should yield and proffer abundance of crops to the farmers during harvest upon several months after the sowing seasons were over.

A critical research into the Hebrew name "Elohim" pays attention to the usage of the plurality of Gods. Therefore, Elohim is the plural form of the singular word El in the Hebrew language. This is actually, why many ancestral traditions have it that it took the collaboration of several Gods to bring about the existence of twin great universes, namely, the physical universe and the spiritual one of course.

I do believe that many a researched fact has proven beyond doubts that the ordinary Ghanaian citizen has been fed with at least a wrong, unfounded and baseless piece of information on account of their past and I mean this historically. Whether or not one believes this, I would say that spirituality is connected to every race of human beings and In simple explanations, I would reveal to us that there is a couple of universes. The Physical Universe and the Spiritual Universe.

The Physical Universe is the very one in which the bodily man lives in or in other words, the universe in which man lives as a sophisticated, scientific individual. The Spiritual Universe is the unseen one in which man dies before entering it. There are only a few groups of men who have direct connections to the spiritual worlds and of course, they do enter into them annually.

Almost all the renowned inventors and scientists have had the privilege of entering them by following secret patterns, ancient scrolls and mystical books. Other physical men have sought for mystical powers to enable them enter into them. The unseen forces dwell in the spiritual universe.

The accounts of Moses, one of Israel's iconic prophets did not mince words when he used the word Elohim in the original Hebrew manuscripts. This is why I do expect the English Bible, and I mean the King James Version of the Bible, which was written in 1611 to have: "In the beginning, the Gods, created the heavens and the earth..." Genesis 1:1. This brief biblical verse unveils some five or six evident theories, videlicet,

The Five Biblically Scientific Theories

"***The Theory of Time***---*"In the beginning..."*
"

"***The Theory of Force***---*"...Gods..." Here, I am using the term Gods owing to the Hebrew name*

Elohim"

"***The Theories of Energy & Friction---*** *"...created..."*"

"***The Theory of Space---****"...the heavens..." Here, I do refer to the Hebrew word Shamayim, which means "the heavens"*
"

"***The Theory of Matter---****"...the Earth..."*"

No human being on this planet Earth gives much more to farmers, and I mean both the traditional or scientific farmers, than what nature does for them. Hence why 'A cob of corn is worth thousand maizes' to them and in the sense of a much more abundant harvest, it is worth million or billion maizes to all and sundry.

This actually depends on how fertile a particular soil is in a specific environment. Geographically, I have observed that some lands have better fertile soil composition than others. And no farmer will practically sow seeds in a laterite yet, seeds have the natural tendencies to germinate in most types of soil.

Other better soils can yield bountiful harvest once farmers have planted in them. The point is that every farmer needs a plentiful harvest hence, why they prefer to sow their seeds in much better soils than others in order to reap a manifold harvest of thousands, millions and so on.

I have with time observed that, wherever weeds grow, any seed is likely to germinate there. So therefore in my country, aside the endowment of the rich mineral reserve imbedded in the lands, the next natural resource that each and every farmer can boast of is the soil.

This has been my personal experience as a subsistent farmer and our lands have hitherto proven to many a farmer.

Every Ghanaian has the natural right of being at least a subsistent farmer and this is so owing to the fact that each parcel of land anywhere and almost everywhere possesses the natural tendencies of allowing almost all seeds to germinate in them.

A practical experiment as a form of exercise can prove to all and sundry about its fertility in a credible way like Tyson's vicious punches to the faces of any of his opponents. In fact, the end result in the course of time can prove this evidence.

Just throw away the seeds of the chilli pepper somewhere irrelevant and you will soon find out that those chilli pepper seeds have germinated there.

To be honest with myself, chilli pepper is expedient in most of our indigenous cuisines such as some local stews and soups: the tomato stew, the garden egg stew, the aubergine stew, groundnut or peanut soups, palm-nut soups, the enumeration is a high one.

Many homes prefer to prepare their local meals with either the fresh chilli pepper, the cooked chilli pepper or better still the dried chilli pepper or even the granulated stuff, and this I do mean in other words, the powdered chilli pepper.

Chilli pepper is as relevant to every farmer as salt is to the miners. Somewhere in this chapter of my book, I stated some five or six theories that have been unveiled by the first verse of the Book of Genesis. I would like to expatiate on them respectively, one after the other.

"FIRST: The Theory of Time"

"In the beginning..."

Prior to the creation and existence of the physical man, who later became what I would later call the scientific man, there was not the existence of time.

The Gods do not operate with time, because time is not existent in the realms of the spiritual.

All deities, irrespective of the tribes, ethnicity or the indigenous people that they are connected to, do not operate from time.

Time was invented for the sake of the physical man. Angelic beings do not exist in time, they all exist out of it. No scientific gadget is capable of calculating how they operate with respect to time, hence, why time is not a factor for their operations.

Demonic beings do not exist around time, they exist out of it. Whatever, spirits do, they do them in time for the sake of the physical man.

With the help of Wikipedia, 'Time' is meant to be the continued sequence of existence and events that occurs in an apparently irreversible succession from the past, through the present, into the future. And before the necessity of time to mankind by the permission of the Gods, there existed the entire period and operations of the Gods, angelic beings, demonic beings, and other unseen forces of the invisible universe.

Perhaps, this was the period which was so-called the "Antediluvian" coined by the famous Thomas Browne. The term can also refer to 'Pre-Diluvian' or 'Pre-Flood' alternatively, and it is the time period chronicled in the Bible between the fall of man and the Genesis flood narrative in biblical cosmology.

"SECOND: The Theory of Force"

"The Supreme GOD and The Gods..."

Although, I have to express here on who "The Gods" are, I would prefer to expatiate on the word "theory". The word "theory" is derived from the Greek "Theos" which means 'God' in the English language. This is why I believe that all theories are connected to spirituality whether small or great, helpful or otherwise.

Importantly, all theories have a huge link with Deities hence, a good theory should be of help to all of mankind. Theories that do not help mankind are not theories, perhaps we can call them different names. Most definitely, they are not theories, if they cannot help man at all. Theories are supposed to be practical enough in bringing to man many a result. I have over the years, spoken to numerous students who often said that they like practicals and avoid theories.

This is happening because man has failed in the aspect of proving to himself that theories are actually practical steps to bringing positive results to mankind. To every theory there is a cause and to each cause there must be an effect. There is no way creation would have taken place if there was no force behind it.

And this very force is a group of Deities. Deities are the Gods that exist as the force behind all of creation. In the ancient belief system of our indigenous people, which is traceable to our ancestry and heritage, we view deity as being both masculine and feminine.

The deity to whom we ascribe the name 'Good Father' is the same we call 'Good Mother'. Deity is both Father and Mother to us, and that is how the issue is to many indigenous Africans. This is why we do not believe in the monotheism but in the pantheism of Gods.

Deity is both singular and plural to us. Deity again, is male and female hence, why there are Gods and Goddesses. The reason being that Deities divide themselves into various avenues in both nature and reality and equally as masculine and feminine.

Deities are not limited to the existence of one God. It is obvious that the original Hebrew manuscripts had and still do have it in revealing Divinity as 'Elohim' to all of mankind and truthfully, 'Elohim' means 'Gods' not 'God' in English. Let me talk about deities as a force or the forces behind the creation of the man in the flesh.

Scientifically, the term "force" is defined as both "a pull" and "a push" hence, the reason for the Gods being behind the existence of Man. The Gods are extremely wise and so collaborated their powers, in order to bring about the appearance of man. Let me be emphatic here.

The Gods did not make man in their image and likeness because they really have no images and likeness; they are image-less and like-less; rather, they made Man their image and likeness because they have no image and likeness. It is wrong for the English language of the Bible to state that, "...God said: 'Let us make man in our image and likeness..." as it appears in the Book of Genesis. It should have been, '...The Gods said, 'Let us (Elohim) make man our image and likeness...'

The Gods are spirit beings and as such deities or spirits do not have images and likeness hence, why they agreed to make Man a bodily structure their image and likeness. The Gods are spiritual beings who have no images and likeness, while men are physical beings who are the images and likeness of the Gods.

It does make sense for spirits who originally do not have an image or likeness to create something bodily to appear as their image and likeness. A bodily structure is an image and likeness of a thought that is unseen.

Human beings are the images and likeness of spirit beings and deities. The Supreme GOD, the Gods, spirit beings, angelic beings, demons among others do not possess an image and likeness hence, why Man is their image and likeness.

Why do spirits, especially, demonic beings desire to possess human beings? The answer is simple. They do not have images hence why they always desire to possess Man.

Man is an image hence why he desires always to operate with Deities, the Gods and Goddesses, the spirits, angelic beings and so on. Just as water finds its way for instance, into a rectangular receptacle to make the receptacle its image, likeness and shape, even so, Deities, GOD with the Gods and the spirits, made Man, the physically scientific Man their image and likeness.

The moment a man bites the dust, or better still, is involved in a fatal accident, the flesh of that man thus, the image and likeness of the Supreme Being, the Gods as well as the spirits, then gives up the ghost and this ghost is certainly the spirit which had for a long time made that man its image.

Deities, the Gods and the spirits constitute the Universal Space, yet they dwell in Man and do appear as men in many forms and appearing in the latter is but their image and likeness. All ghosts are invisible and image-less (no exact image) and the moment any human being is said to have seen one it implies that, that ghost made a previous body its image in appearance. I would explain further on this somewhere in this book.

"THIRD: The Theories of Energy and Friction"

"Created (thus Made)..."

When I was in the elementary school, classmates often stated that, "Energy is the ability to do work" and so it means that for work to be done, one requires an energy. I prefer to define friction in the words of Wikipedia: Friction is the force resisting the relative motion of solid surfaces, fluid layers, and material elements sliding against each other.

There are several types of friction and dry friction is one of those. Dry Friction is simply, a force that opposes the relative lateral motion of two solid surfaces in contact. The Supreme GOD with the Gods therefore, collaborated their energies in order to bring about all of creation.

It took Them synergy to bring Nature into existence. Yes, it takes synergy to create something when people are the subject matter. Energy on the part of oneself is as important as synergy on the parts of collaborated individuals. When people combine their energies as one, it is revealed in what is called synergy.

The energy of an individual person is needful in respect of what he wants to do everyday. It was in respect of the past tense of the verb "created" that both "energy" and "friction" simultaneously took place. In many a way, the scientific terms energy and friction work hand in hand. They are the twin forceful elements of all deities in making physical creation with the existence of the man as the unique image and likeness of the Gods possible.

"FOURTH: The Theory of Space"

"The Heavens (thus all the Seven Heavens)"

The word "heavens" in English refers to the Hebrew word "Shamayim" which is often and always plural yet the English Bible contains in itself both the singular and plural forms. The heavens are the space and these are image-less and measureless. Space cannot be measured and so are the heavens.

What the heavens refer to the space so does. Everything which the physical man has a sight of is actually existent in space. Everything hangs and dwells within space, hence why the scientific man cannot measure space with any scientific gadgets or methodologies.

The heavens are all the Seven Heavens which start with the Physical Heaven in which Man subdues and takes dominion over; the Spiritual Universe which contains the Six Heavens which are the Spiritual Realms of the Princes of Light, the Princes of Darkness, their Powers and Principalities, the unseen vast realms of spiritual wickedness that are resident in high places, the colossal and vast dimensions of measureless heights, depths, and widths within which all things exist and move, such as the physical or the scientific man, all animals, and the rest of the created things of nature, except for the Gods, Spiritual Beings, Angelic Beings and many more of the spiritual realms, but to state only a few.

The Sun which is practically huger and bigger than most of the planetary bodies and elements exists in space or 'the heavens' and when I use the term 'the heavens' I do not refer to where basically, the physical man believes that the Supreme GOD exists with the innumerable company of His Angels as written in the Bible.

I use the above-mentioned term to imply 'Space' which is the measureless and gigantic dimensions of heights, depths, widths and so on.

All planetary bodies such as Jupiter, Mars, Venus, Uranus, Earth, Mercury, Neptune and what have you, hang individually within space, yet the space is never replete with them.

In fact, the space cannot and will never be full of all created things, whether the ones that do exist or the ones that are yet to appear in existence.

Even if the sand particles of the shores of the seas, were made to appear as significantly, the big things of nature, space would be far more than enough to contain and inhabit them in their respective, varied numbers, for gigantically, measureless are the heavens, thus, space while imagelessly, ubiquitous and audacious are all the Gods, whose tangible image as well as likeness is but the physically, scientific man, who governs or controls or regulates all the various realms, whether they be invisible or visible, from the matter called the planet Earth.

Any and every spiritual being, which desires to appear in the realms of the physical, such as the Earth, for instance, can only do so as a form of matter or otherwise, a substantial element of matter in space, which the Earth itself is known for suspending in it as other giant elements do.

Any visible element whether small or large, huge or dwarf-like, is a part and parcel of matter, which dwells and suspends in space. All the invisible elements whether spiritual thrones, principalities, powers or the Gods themselves, who altogether, created the twin universes, namely, the spiritual universe and the physical universe, are actually space itself.

I have stated that there is a couple of universes, thus, the spiritual and the physical universes of which the former is the invisible one yet it is a part and parcel of space, while the latter being the visible one, dwells and hangs in space. All the elements that do exist including man himself, have not occupied a portion of space that is up to one percent of all of it.

"*FIFTH: The Theory of Matter*"

"The Earth (thus the Terrestrial Plane)"

My moments at school in class one day were filled with much excitement and laughter amidst my colleagues in respect of one of the popular subtopics in Science. The teacher began by telling her class on what "Matter" means and desired to know what each student of her class had to say that day. I would like to express my comprehension on what really "Matter" means to me here.

"Matter" is simply anything of existence which can be seen and touched, though others cannot be touched by reason of their distances in space. These things that constitute matter occupy portions of space in our physical universe. Again, these things possess different weights in addition to their varied widths, depths, breadths and heights in respect of space.

The Earth is mentioned in the Bible as the major example of matter which exists in space. Most definitely, the planet Earth has a gigantic amount of weight besides its size as in what comprises its width, height, depth and breadth altogether.

It is quite obvious that each of the things that we often see and touch in nature, is practically, a form of matter, as it owns weight and can also occupy a portion of space in the universal space, as other large elements do.

By practical observation personally, I can state that without matter, the universal space would be void or empty. It takes each and every form of matter to beautify the universal space. And owing to this, therefore, matter is as important as beauty is to every female gender.

If the Gods had ignored or neglected matter in their creation, the whole physical universe would have been full of emptiness and with large amounts of vacuum. Man himself, who invented the idea of what matter is, is a significant form of matter.

There are things of matter that are as lively as man is in space. All living things are parts and parcels of matter and practically all non-living things also are parts of matter. The reason being that they also possess weights and can occupy space in respect of the universal space.

> ***"I am Hyperion and so therefore, I am 'Making It Now!'***
>
> ***You are Hyperion and so therefore, You are 'Making It Now!'***
>
> ***"***

CHAPTER FOUR

MANY A DROP OF RAIN DRENCHES A WHOLE BODY

"MANY A DROP OF RAIN DRENCHES A WHOLE BODY"

I was born in a suburb which still has numerous hustlers who go through thick and thin to make ends meet. I went through quite a number of hustling activities while growing up in Accra.

I want to talk about where I grew up before narrating to you on where I am currently. This place was and still is an impoverished suburb that is situated in the Greater-Accra Region where the Capital City is located.

I want this local vicinity to gain some sort of popularity via this book and this can only be attained as countless individuals read their own copies of the book.

This place is called 'Maamobi' and there is a particular, public Polyclinic here that has for a long time had its fair share of prominence. This is where I was born over four decades ago, in June of 1978.

Coincidentally, I was born the same year in which the famous South African journalist and activist, Stephen Bantu Biko died. This automatically, allowed me to bear the name of this great person as mentioned a while ago.

Most of my early childhood friends called me Steve Biko of Soweto and I was enthused by this special name. It made me feel unique anywhere I went whether far or near. Several times my close friends made it some fun to often say that I could become the next Member of Parliament for my local district.

In fact, I like being popular but not on the grounds of some so-called dirty politics practised in the Ghanaian environment currently. So many people in my country make mountains out of molehills in terms of acquiring political powers and stardom, yet after the acquisition of power, they plunge the poor masses into the ditches of more abject poverty than they were previously.

A chunk of diabolical persons had killed a handful of their political opponents in order to simply gain some amount of political powers only to exercise these powers on the poor masses who voted them into many political offices and positions.

Since the constitutional year of 1992, many aspiring politicians have gone through the eye of a needle to usurp political positions, all in the name of some partisan politics and others have had the privilege of being plenipotentiaries via the nomination and direct appointment of the government of the day.

They premeditate all sorts of schemes to see their opponents lose to them. They have for many a year played politics like football or soccer. Soccer or football has hitherto created numerous rivalries and enemies.

To a large extent, they have come to accept that all of their actions and premeditated plans have a close connection with democracy. I know a scanty number of my childhood friends who became the enemies of other friends owing to partisan politics.

They hurt, wound and even kill their opposing friends during political campaigns and elections. In such periods abhorrence and hatred becomes the order of the day for all and sundry. I have until now been neutral during political campaigns and elections.

No single friend of mine who has been committed to partisan politics ever knew the party I voted for. To be honest, I never voted the presidential candidates of one particular party every four years. I voted based on what words that a presidential candidate said and perhaps, if what he said really made some sense to me, then he became the best choice for me that period.

Now politics has become quite a disappointment to many a Ghanaian citizen. The commonest of citizens has become fed up with the way some once-trusted politicians turned out to be. It has become a game-chain which every presidential candidate must follow in order to gain votes and subsequently some amount of power.

After the acquisition of power, the next thing to be acquired is wealth or riches or money. I would add that one of the most famous tools which for several centuries has been used to brainwash the multitudes in Africa, especially, is not only democracy but Christianity.

Christianity has used a prominent informative strategy which is contained in just one book, to brainwash, thwart our traditions and customs and also to wipe away our heritage, culture and great African history.

This book contains several bits and pieces of 'cut and paste' historical facts of many black people per se, and it does discard their ancient belief systems and the sundry historical events of the realities of human beings as they walked with the Gods, aliens, the Nephilims or the giants. It was the aliens who had appeared to teach us the high technological artistry and innovations which we know today in the world, before they left us.

It is quite a high time, most of those realities and truths were revealed to the world. It is obvious that a few people all over the world know about such realities. In India, many ancient archeological facts are there to prove; in Mexico as well as in other parts of the globe.

Personally, a number of the foreign movies which I watched when I was but a child, had already revealed to me most of the hidden facts to the rest of the world.

They enter into the door of politics as poor politicians and come out of the same as rich politicians, ministers, parliamentarians or otherwise.

Politics and power brainwash them in such a way that they cannot trace the path to their original routes and roots. I imply "routes" here in terms of the original "pathways" to their provenance and "roots" by reason of their "sources" or better still "where they had begun their journeys" which in essence directs to their "provenances".

They forfeit their being genuine, patriotic, loyal and the likes towards their nation and fellow citizens. Their voices clamour for peace but their actions wage wars and tribal sentiments. Their hearts yearn to help the poor masses but their way of life oppresses them into impoverishment.

They stood before the masses on the day of political campaigns and elections on lean bellies and roam the streets of Accra and elsewhere on potbellies and stout bodies. The feelings of the pains and agonies of the poor masses are in their hearts and on their lips yet their actions penalize them in the jail of poverty.

They maltreat the poor citizens with iron hands and fists of rage. A drop of water matters equally as drops of the same. In a nutshell, the actions and lifestyles of our politicians have been that of little drops of water which make a thousand liters. A full bucket of water alone cannot fill a tank to the brim.

Certainly, it takes a number of buckets full of water to fill the entire tank to the brim. Evil prevails over good in bits and pieces, hence why the little amounts of bad attitudes of our leaders in various parts of Africa, lead to a heightened corruption and of course, a hugely bad attitude in display.

On the condition that evil men and women rule the nooks and crannies of their countries as well as some parts of the African continent at large, the inhabitants, who are mainly Africans, are those who suffer the most in all of this transpiration.

They are oppressed and suppressed to accept evil deeds as the standard of living for themselves and by this I would recall that the Reggae dude Robert Nesta Marley had once sung that, "You can fool some people sometimes, but you can't fool all the people all the time"

The era of awareness and critical surveillance, by this I mean watchfulness, coupled with some realization in respect of the failed promises and utterances of the politicians are nigh to everyone. And it is nearer to every individual in such a wonderful way that none of them wants to be fooled this time around.

All the actions and premeditated plans of the politicians have become the little drops of water which make a thousand liters. This in other words can appear as their cups are full and filled. And the moment a jar is fully filled, it begins to overflow and the water gets wasted.

African leaders had begun depredation in small amounts of cash from the National Treasury, until it culminated into the embezzling and stealing of large amounts of money from the same National Treasury. They had begun stealing little drops of money and so they feel that it is a high time they commenced a clear theft on gigantic amounts of money.

They crave for bigger and better material benefits in respect of their selfish interests. When and if they go into the Parliament House at all, they no longer discuss the welfare and wellbeing of the country and its poor citizens. They always remember to discuss themselves, hence, why as often as possible, they increase their remuneration from one zero to the other.

Practically, they increase their salaries from for instance, USD100.00 to USD1,000.00 and from here to USD10,000.00 and so on until they have felt that it is good enough for each and everyone of them as politicians, parliamentarians and ministers in political positions.

They are eager to live more-than-being- comfortable lives until there is a huge wastage and surplus to spend on concubines or 'side-chicks' or slay queens whether they are living abroad or back home. All of these are the little drops of bad attitudes and behaviors that cripple the arms and legs of our National Treasury every now and then.

I have come to observe that any man who yearns or desires to become a millionaire or billionaire does a number of investments here and there; and all of these amount to huge sums of money and gradually he becomes a millionaire. It is a part and parcel of a natural reality that the small 'spoon-fulls' of food amount to one's being fully fed and satisfied.

It takes time to be fed to satisfaction; and whether or not you wish to eat quickly or slowly, it still takes time to be fully satisfied with the meal. Is it not a fact that a drop of water cannot drench one's whole body? I foresee a period of time nearer than we can see, and where the poor masses will mobilize themselves in unity to ousted all the individual leaders who do not help or discuss the interest of the citizens.

This is the time and we are 'Making It Now!' no matter what it takes to achieve this. Indeed, persuasion has failed us, hence force must and should be applied on anyone who does not help the poor masses.

There comes a specific time when the poor masses will take away and do away with any systems and dictates of the Constitution which does not allow for the progress of the citizens. The youths will arise to the occasion, 'Making It Now!' and if it behoves on them to take the bulls by the horns, they will be glad to do so for the benefit of all.

This paradigm shift should be one that demands a forward-ever approach with a backward-never attitude. Nobody will sweep your house clean for you until you have agreed to hire them in order to pay them what they deserve. Only a few will sweep others‘ house on the grounds of charity and benevolence.

The rest will do so on the basis of being paid some money. The new 'Nelson Mandelas‘ should rise up and create a better world for their posterity. The new 'Stephen Bikos‘ should clamor for peace in the midst of their financial constraints and crises not leaving their respective, individual countries to rot in riots and petty fights.

They must do all that they can to settle matters in order to move their countries ahead or forward. I urge the African youths to soar on their wings like the eagles do in the air in the midst of all chaotic situations, as the new 'Barack Obamas' for the continent of Africa especially. We are 'Making It Now!'

> ***"Whatever and whoever I am, you are. I am Hyperion and so therefore, I am 'Making It Now!'"***

> ***"A TRIP OF THOUSAND KILOMETERS OWES ALL TO A SINGLE STEP"***

As a teenager and this I mean at about 15 years old, my granny bit the dust at the age of 89, in 1993. Almost all my siblings had put up with our grandma, except for my youngest sister, Catherine, who lived with my mother in Lagos, Nigeria.

I observed that my grandmother was quite kindhearted and benevolent in a way that her generosity extended towards a large number of the poor and hungry who resided in the neighborhood at the time. She really loved people and was never discriminating against all who beckoned her for some reasonable assistance.

She was always willing to support others at her own expense. And owing to this, I know how to love others at the expense of myself. Many people are selfish and those who propose love to you do so because of what they could accrue from you. Try to put them through at least a single test and you would be stunned that they had pretended to you for quite awhile.

A lot of children lived with my grandma, and most of them were the children of some poor parents living in some villages then. Today, a number of those villages are now towns and almost being cities.

About a half of those children who stayed with my grandma were adopted by her and so it was necessary that they had to live with us. The rest of the children were either her nieces or grandchildren. I still do recollect that I was her only grandson in her home.

I grew up being in the midst of many opposite sexes and I mean teenage girls. To be honest, I learnt a handful of things and endured some attitudinal acts from my siblings and most of my cousins.

I was like the most favorite grandchild of granny. The reason being that, I attended the best school in those days before leaving for the Government's cluster of schools in the suburb.

My grandmother was a genuine prophetess who never took or extorted money from anyone who consulted with her. She never presented any case to those many individuals who visited her for help to take money. I had learnt from her that, "...freely, have ye received, freely give..." and this was her lifestyle.

Many indigenes came to her for healing and her attitude showed that she relied completely upon a higher source of power, Who is often called "Father" by her in most of her prayers.

She once taught me how to pray by saying, "Jesus Christ" repeatedly if I really do not know what to say. At least there are some of those children who are adults today, who would attest to this narration of mine as being true.

Each time anyone of them saw me they reminisced about some past occurrences and numerous of the healings that people received through her.

She never rushed into doing things and we were admonished by her to take a cue from being patient and kind towards people without discrimination or any atom of vice against others.

She spoke out many predictions that came to pass, hence, why many people believed in the kind of deity she served. In fact, she worked with a higher deity.

I say this because, she told me when she would leave this earth and it happened just as she had predicted. She once told me that, "Single steps are tantamount to a mile" and this I had lived with until now, knowing that gradually, I will meet up with my helper who has been connected to me to help my destiny.

I have hitherto believed in destiny. Indeed, a trip of a thousand kilometers owes all to a single step and is a wise statement one can live by.

After all, "Rome was not built in a day" for I did realize several years ago that what really makes a real man in the midst of all the experiences of life, is actually the bits and pieces of all that he had endured and been through thoroughly.

By this reality then a real man is not evident in the physical stature of a man's anatomy and most definitely it should not be seen in his muscular endurance nor in his abilities to combat against others to the point of defeating them all; it is seen in how enduring that man is when it comes to life's experiences.

His ability to endure hunger or starvation; his ability to be unshakable in respect of the turbulence of the storms of life; his tendency to struggle through life and to overcome whatsoever that life brings as a surprise to him.

Let me relate this to technology here. Technology has evolved with respect to times and seasons over the years. A flashback to at least a decade, in view of the existence of Apple's iPhone then cannot be compared to the state of technology of today's iPhone.

All phones irrespective of the brands are much better with respect to technology than those of several years ago. For a long time, we have seen for ourselves, that technology has provided several steps for man towards a forward direction in the sense that today's technological innovations and advancements hitherto build upon yester years' technology.

In order for man to take a huge stride in technology, he must amble a few steps backwards first, to be able to move forward with technology. In a simple analysis, we have observed that Macro Technology has paved the way for Micro Technology while the latter has chartered a beautiful course for Nano Technology.

Many manufactured products over the years have become handy and portable for customers in the sense that the sizes of avalanche products have dropped to become much smaller than the previous ones.

There is never a set record in the world by one man which cannot be broken by another man. Old records are meant to be broken by men and women alike for new ones to be set by the same.

In biblical times, the nine-foot-tall giant in the person of Goliath, the Philistine, perhaps had set many records during the days, until, the teenage Israelite boy, David appeared on the scene to challenge him.

The teenager's challenge against the giant was not one that made any sense to all and sundry, especially, the young Israelite soldiers who had vowed to defend and save their beloved nation, Israel.

During those days, Israel had a united kingdom ruled by a humble man called Saul, who was as huge as Goliath the giant. King Saul with his battalion of soldiers had failed to take on the Philistine Giant.

However, the young boy, David, who was both a good shepherd and a fearless hunter decided to face the uncircumcised Philistine warrior.

David by the backing of Yahweh Sabaoth of Israel, defeated Goliath and then decapitated him right on that spot. This young man then set the newest and latest record ever in the history of all the wars of many a nation, both in Israel as well as in the neighboring states or kingdoms.

Many a company of women had chanted and sung songs to hail David to the extent that those songs drew the rapt attention of King Saul but into an infuriating, extreme jealousy against David.

After all, why should he be extremely jealous to the point of trying many a time to exterminate the young man?

The young man had several chances to have assassinated his king in order to set another record. His first attempt was quite a great opportunity to have assassinated the king of the United Kingdom of Israel. David refused to murder King Saul on many accountable grounds.

Wise men have often said that, "...the most constant aspect of nature and life is nothing else but change" and indeed, change is constant. This is so in view of the constant dynamics of change.

The minutest aspect of nature and life go through metamorphoses, in other words changes. Change has become the perfection which man hankers after, every day.

Several years ago, domestic animals such as dogs, cats, goats, sheep and other animals which have become pets to man, could not buy for their masters and I mean man as their master, from the markets and shopping malls.

However, in the recent past until now, the dogs especially, have been trained well enough to go on errands to the markets and malls, in order to purchase many items for the home. It has become quite easy for dogs to do so in this current situation of technology.

Dogs have become highly circumspect to the extent that when they go to the markets to buy items they know what exactly to buy for their masters in respect of the home. Let a vendor dare to put the wrong items in their baskets and they would begin to bark at her.

Other dogs would not bark but for them, they would not take an inch away from the vendor until she puts into the basket the exact items. With the help of man, a dog has been able to travel to the Moon and returned successfully without problems.

Yesterday's man is quite below the standard of today's man, hence why today's man believes more in actions than in words. He accepts the fact that if it must or should be done, it must be done now. He is bent on 'Making It Now!' and so he does it.

Today's man is the man of actions while yesterday's man was the man of more words than actions. If our world must achieve a high level of perfection in respect of technological innovations and sophistication, 'Making It Now!' should be the agenda. He is ready to 'Making It Now!'

A certain famous prophet of the nation of Israel had a cordial relationship with one of the most renowned royals of his people. This great prophet was commanded by the God of Israel to christen a newborn baby boy with the name of Jedidiah, which means 'Beloved of the LORD' and could also mean 'Friend of God'

This newborn baby boy later was Solomon, the same man who became one of Israel's most beloved royals. His parents had been the then king of the United Kingdom of Israel like himself, and his mother was one of the most beautiful women of Israel.

This beautiful woman had been coveted by the then king of Israel from one of his most trusted and loyal soldiers, Uriah, to be his wife. Solomon, who later became the last of the kings of the United Kingdom of Israel, was to be christened Jedidiah, however, the former name became highly renowned instead.

He was the second son of King David and Bathsheba was his mother. Before David became the cherished king of his people, he had mustered courage from the pieces of his many experiences, first as a young shepherd boy through to his becoming a great hero, in respect of his triumphing over Goliath, the Philistine Giant.

David's royalty owed so much more to the slices of all the experiences which he had gathered from childhood until adulthood. His being one of the greatest kings of his own country did not just occur overnight. It took several years of numerous experiences to be a great dude.

And his being an astute warrior owed all to those days when he summoned courage and bravery to launch attacks at ferocious animals like the lion and bear which had come to devour his father's flock on the fields. David was fearless to the extent that this aspect of his attitude helped him climb the ladder of heights.

One day my dad asked me a tricky question, and so he then said, "Son, which of these two, will you choose;' Wisdom or riches?" I was just 17 years old then when he asked me this question and this was in the year, 1995. I frankly answered, "Dad, I choose riches!" My answer was an exclamatory sentence. My dad was highly surprised and wondered; owing to this he asked me, "Why son, do you choose riches over wisdom?"

I then explained to him why I had chosen riches with respect to his question. I made my dad understand that, I already had wisdom so therefore it was not expedient for me to choose wisdom when I already have it. I chose riches because it was what neither my dad nor myself, his son had then.

It was necessary for me to aspire to be rich hence why I chose riches over wisdom based on his question. He later lauded me for my wisdom and said, "Son, you're wise and so you decided to choose what you didn't have" It is so fascinating but important for one to always choose what he does not have at all.

Many a time, wise men have chosen wisdom, when they really should not have chosen it. It is quite discreet for a rich dude to seek after what he does not have at all. Wise people always hanker for what they do not possess.

King Solomon, observed that his father, from whom he had succeeded being the heir to the throne and kingdom, had amassed wealth and riches altogether, hence, there was nothing in life that he really required except for wisdom to manage the inherited wealth and riches of the kingdom coupled with the steering of the many affairs of his own people.

As their king, the only factor which he was bereft of as far as his kingdom and his people were concerned was the availability of wisdom and understanding to govern the Israelites. It must be comprehended that, King Solomon, had asked the LORD God of Israel for wisdom and understanding owing to the fact that he was bereft of them.

Money was not his problem and of course, wealth and riches were not his problem too. Whatsoever he wanted as far as wealth is concerned he got it at a simple command in his great and large kingdom.

This was how King Solomon was well able to rule over his own people, the Israelites. All of these culminated into the huge peace and safety that his people and wonderful nation Israel enjoyed for over four decades during his reign.

Neighboring kingdoms revered and respected Solomon, the wise king. The Queen of Sheba did not come to King Solomon in view of his wealth and riches or prosperity; she came from a distant land only to see for herself, the kind of unique wisdom with which King Solomon ruled his kingdom and people.

She was thrilled and amazed at his wisdom and understanding. This was what brought about the king's prominence for many years.

As I was growing up into adulthood, wisdom played a significant role in my daily life. I had and still do have wisdom, hence, why my desire is not to acquire wisdom but to hanker after wealth and riches as well as prosperity.

Man always must seek after what he really does not have at all. In discretion, if and when a man chooses foolishness, we must see that in the light of his lack of it.

Life's experiences have taught me that the man who already has wisdom will not have a serious necessity for what he already has, hence, why he should choose something else. For instance, a wise man who does not have foolishness must be willing to choose it.

It does not make any sense however, foolishness is helpful to him. Many individuals who became different from others realized that it was relevant for them to seek after what others do not have in order for them to look different from the lot.

I always seek to appear different from my colleagues and friends, because being the same with them does not allow for greatness. The Englishman says, "Necessity is the mother of invention" hence, what a man does not have it becomes a necessity for him so then he goes all out to look for it no matter what happens. Some years down the road, I observed that almost everyone appeared the same and so commonness became the order of the day in those days.

I then realized that it was quite importunate for me to appear and look different from all of them. Being the same means looking like someone else. And people appearing the same is said to be a common phenomenon.

Similarities do not and cannot chart a course which leads men into being extraordinary, but differences do help men to a large extent. Differences are the pacesetters of a man's world. When and if a man is different, he is seen as being an extraordinary gentleman.

Similarities are relatively tantamount to the existence of an ordinary fellow, while differences make an extraordinary gentleman appear out of the way.

The difference between an ordinary man and an extraordinary man is simply the existence of the word 'extra' attached to the latter. The word 'extra' is the difference.

The 'extra factor' to a man's attitude is what actually makes him a much better individual than another man who is ordinary. Moreover, the difference between a prayerful man and a prayerless man is revealed in the fact that the former is full of prayer while the latter is less of it.

The common factor between them is that they both have the word prayer attached to their description. Commonness as well as similarities do not and cannot breed extraordinary men.

What breeds extraordinary men is differences and discrepancies. This is why it is quite vital for any individual to be a man or woman of difference in the midst of a common-voiced, common-viewed as well as a common-opinionated men and women in every society and country. In other words, a person with a huge difference grasps more followers than what common-voiced men can gather in any society and community.

There are densely populated, common individuals who lurk and linger behind various parts of our society. It makes sense to have an individual who emerges as one man who possesses a different voice amidst the rest, in order for the same to make a hugely clear difference among the lot.

In biblical era, the Pharisees followed almost all the core traditions of their fathers and so commonness was the order of the day, until, Jesus, the Christ appeared suddenly to make a difference hence, why he emerged as one man on several platforms during his day to have more followers than what the Pharisees had. He felt that if there was anything to be done during his days, it should be done as soon as possible hence, 'Making It Now!' was all the results which were required and sought after by the ignorant multitude or masses.

In every early society, a number of men and women followed after the traditions and customs of their forefathers and predecessors whether they be good or otherwise. They never felt to have ample time to think through those traditions and customs of their forefathers until a man or woman emerges who possesses a different opinion to save situations.

Many traditions and customs did not help a number of posterity until one indigenous individual appears to change the course of things. Being different is highly recommended, since it helps to allow for a huge difference in the society.

In the historical events of my country, Ghana, when it used to be called the Gold Coast, a renowned political party called the United Gold Coast Convention, emerged as a single voice to claim independence for their people, where they believed that "Self-government in the shortest possible time" could be the last straw which would break the camel's back, until one of the first Big Six Men, in the person of Dr. Kwame Nkrumah, who was one of the learned, indigenous men of the Gold Coast, emerged to differ from the rest of his colleagues.

He, Dr Osagyefo Francis Kwame Nkrumah, Ghana's first Prime Minister and President, opposed the rest by declaring that,

> ***"*"Self-government now"*"***

Was to be the order of the day at the expense of :

> ***"*"Self-government in the shortest possible time".*"***

Many of the then Gold Coast Ghanaians followed his view and later with his own new Big Six Team of famous men such as Dr Kwame Nkrumah himself, Komla Gbedemah, Kojo Botsio, Krobo Edusei, Nathaniel Welbeck and presumably, Paa Grant who founded the previous party called the UGCC.

He was a rich merchant who on many occasions may have supported or sponsored members of the previous Big Six Team yet he was not a member of the team. In case he was not the new member of Nkrumah's Big Six Team then I do not know whose name it was as a member of the new Big Six Team who led us to independence that night.

I cannot remember now what one of my grandfathers had told me yet, all went ahead to claim independence for all of us on that special day at the Independence Square, on the 6th of March, 1957. He became the first Prime Minister and President of Ghana until he was overthrown in his absence on the 24th day of February, 1966, by Lieutenant Colonel Emmanuel K. Kotota.

Just as the appearance of Jesus, the Christ, brought a huge difference during his days to disturb the views of the famous Pharisees, so also was the case of Dr. Kwame Nkrumah, against his former, political enemies, in the early days of colonialism in the then Gold Coast, now Ghana.

It behoves on the current posterity to be different at the expense of what our predecessors had done so that moving forward will not be any more of a problem than it had been. We seem to be refusing to move forward as a people. It is therefore, high time we started taking some huge steps in 'Making It Now' because it is the only solution for any man and this allows for a clear difference.

> ***"I am the Man who walks on high as the Son of God. What I am that is exactly what you are. We are Hyperion and so therefore, I am 'Making It Now!'"***

CHAPTER FIVE

ONE MAN'S TRASH IS ANOTHER'S TREASURE

"*One Man's Trash Is Another's Treasure* "

I would like to begin this chapter by stating one of my personal quotes here: 'To the common individual, a prudent king declares plain words, while to the wise man, he utters only proverbs'.

On several platforms, the words of many philosophers sounded as difficult to be understood by others who were usually the masses as well as the huge crowds who thronged at them to listen to their opinions and wise words.

Most of those ancient philosophers as well as wise teachers uttered wise words to the multitude who often came to hear them speak. Moreover, many of those philosophers or wise teachers, chose to speak in plain words to the crowd listening to them.

In the same vein, the biblical records reveal that Jesus, the Christ, spoke to the crowd in wise, but plain words to the masses yet he declared proverbs to his followers.

Sometimes, those who did not understand him asked why he spoke to them in proverbs and not in just plain words.

In simple terms and this often times, he expounded to the multitude or crowd that, he would rather speak in wise but plain words, while to his followers who were probably as wise as he was, he would deliberately utter proverbs.

> “*The word "philosophy" is etymologically, a Greek word which had been anglicized over centuries. It emanates from the Greek word, "philosophia". This word moved into Latin then to French before finally being anglicized by speakers of Middle English Language.*”

One can derive two words "phileo" which means "love" and "sophia" meaning "wisdom" in English. In short, ‘philosophia’ is a phrase which reads: ’the love of or for wisdom‘ in the Queen’s lingua franca. In ancient times, philosophers were actually a bunch of ’lovers of wisdom‘ or men who pursued and sought after wisdom for the love of it.

For many years, I appeared to be an idiotic person on several occasions only to learn some didactic lessons in life and by so doing, I learnt a lot from experiences and then gained much wisdom. Life offers a vast array of experiences to those who tread along its paths.

Yes, this is where David once said, "...though I walk through the valley of the shadow of death, I shall fear no evil..." In short, I was bereft of discretion many a time, until, I learnt from life with its wisdom on how to be wise in a lot of ways. I do own a lot of appreciation and indebtedness to life with its experiences so far.

Several years down the road have culminated into my acquisition of enriched wisdom to the core and this has gone a long way to help me. I was seeking to be affluent and prominent in the society. I had undergone various experiences through the use of observations and so with all of these, I gained great wisdom.

I had a sedentary one day, and watched the outgoings and incomings of many foreigners who had come from other parts of Africa, such as Mali, Niger, Burkina Faso and Somalia precisely.

Usually, these foreigners went round the nooks and crannies of our country in search of scrubs and petty metallic substances which were to us supposedly of no use at all. I did not fathom why these metallic scrubs and plastic substances should be of great importance to them when in actual fact they were not significant to me as well as others.

But, little did I know that one man's trash is another's treasure. With the various trashy substances or scrubs they had collected from many areas, they made huge sums of money to build mansions in their home countries, such as in Mali, Somalia, Niger, Burkina Faso and more.

Most of the time, indigenous people abandoned metallic substances or scrubs on either refuse damp sites or somewhere in the corners of the neighborhoods. Most Ghanaians never bothered to sell off scrubs to these guys but rather would allow these foreigners as mentioned earlier to come for them for free. This took place for several years until we all realized that these scrub guys had made money from the collection of scrubs and so we had no other choice than to at least sell such scrubs off to them for whatever good use they might need them.

These foreigners often times pushed around metal carriages in each neighborhood, in order to collect scrubs of varied types, such as small metallic substances, plastic substances and so on and so forth.

Personally, I never sold scrubs to any of them, but rather I would allow them to collect them for free until one day, while peeping through my old window, I saw a usual guy put his hand into his pocket to bring out a huge amount of cash and this was all the clue to knowing that such various trashy substances were their treasure.

I was highly surprised on seeing such a huge amount of money, because my previous impression about them had been that was they are beggarly and uneducated. Well in reality, quite enough beggars are bound to become givers later on in their lives, while most uneducated people have been able to build a lot of educational centres for their communities and so I had been wrong all the time by what I saw that they were beggarly.

People like me, despised them for a long period of time until I observed that they have cash. This was what moved to be start selling off scrubs to them. They often get pick up scrubs on refuse damp sites, isolated camps, dilapidated areas, and many more.

Indeed, it is not good enough to judge people until you get to know them. I realized it was extremely significant to do a thorough research about scrubs so that I would no longer sell them off cheaply to these scrub guys. They usually, would like to buy various types of scrubs cheaply from people each time they came around.

I had the privilege of befriending one of the scrub guys, whose name should be Ali, as I often called him. I had a great connection with him in a way that he found it necessary to reveal vital pieces of information to me in respect of scrub business. After all, Ali has become my friend, so I felt that he should have the scrubs from me either for free or cheaply.

Sometimes, I called on him to let him know that I had been hard up and so I required some financial assistance from him. He never refused to help me as the case usually is that he was willing to help me anytime. The point being that, the Englishman often says, "One good turn deserves another" and after all, Ali and I have become friends ever since.

Without a proper and careful observation any man will not regard scrub business as a lucrative business until he thoroughly gets into it. The individual appearances of these scrub guys do not appeal to motivate others like me for instance to go into it.

Often times, scrub business is being despised and discredited on several platforms. However, and in all of these, I have known that one man's trash is another's treasure, as far as this scrub business is mentioned. The next lucrative business which is despised and rejected by almost everyone is waste materials and plastics that have been thrown away.

I would like to entail food waste and fecal matters into this lucrative business. It sure is lucrative because, a man from one of the famous churches has been popular owing to general waste collections. When he began this business most people like myself in the neighborhood and country, saw him as an absurd guy and for lack of a better phrase, we said, "... he's out of his mind..." until, he started making huge amount of cash from it.

Until today, he has multiplied his cash and has offered employed to a large percentage of the unemployed youth in my country. This man had begun with trash and now he owns the treasure. Whatever, he wants he gets it. He owns and steers the official affairs of a group of companies called the Jospong Group of Companies, in almost every part of my country, Ghana.

One of the several biblical verses warns all of us, "...not to despise little or humble beginnings..." for no great nation today had begun as a great nation but as a small one. Great Britain today, had begun as a small Britain until with time, it became known as great.

"STRATEGY PLAYS A ROLE TOWARDS GREATNESS"

The greatness of a nation is not evident in its population but in its power to achieve results. Great Britain has for many years overpowered various nations whose population are twice or three times more than Great Britain's.

Strategy plays a major role in overcoming other countries when it comes to wars, tribal wars and conflicts, in order to be projected highly and described as being great. The term "strategy" is derived indirectly from the Classic and Byzantine ancient roots somewhere in the year 330 AD (Anno Domini) and it hails from a Greek word "strategos" which means "general" in English.

It is said and often noted that while the term is originally credited to the Grecians, in other words, the Greeks, no Grecian ever made a verbal use of it or used the word at all. I do believe that the Greek word "strategos" is meant to suit a noun in respect of a human being rather than an abstract noun in view of what we do not see.

So therefore, a "general" is an officer of high rank in the armies, and in some nations' air forces, space forces, and marines or naval infantry. In some usages the term "general officer" refers to a rank above colonel.

In most of the battles the biblical Israelite nation conquered and defeated numerous warring states by the deployment of generals like Joshua, for instance, to fight against their enemies, rather than just using strategy to overcome the wars and she, Israel, did not achieve this great feat in respect of her population but, in view of also, her power and strategy in the so-called wars and battles. Israel was and still is strategic when it comes to wars.

In fact, on accounts of ancient times, most of those warring nations which Israel had defeated were more populated and more prominent than Israel. In the biblical story of the last born son of Jesse, which was David, it was immediately, observed that David, the young teenager was smart and strategic as a teenager and this was how he defeated Goliath the Philistine Giant.

He managed to decapitate him and this led to the presence of fear amongst the soldiers within the Philistine army. Fear again arrested the neighboring states and so David, when he became King triumphed over them easily.

He conquered every neighboring state to the point that King Solomon, his son, who took the throne as his heir apparent and successor, would not have to wage any more wars against neighboring states because those states had paid taxes in varied forms to his father David, the king before he took over from him.

This was why these neighboring states regarded King Solomon as a sovereign king to them. Likewise Abraham, one of the first patriarchs, when he had begun his journey towards a certain point, he settled at a place which was originally not the best yet by his walk with the God of Israel, fought and defeated at least fourteen great kings who had their kingdoms.

These great kings did not fight individually against Abraham but collaborated in a coalition against Abraham. These kings had taken hostage of Lot with his family and so it demanded that Abraham on hearing that his nephew had been taken away, had to prepare three hundred and eighteen of his fighting men to launch an attack against those fourteen kings.

Abraham with his fighting men pursued them until they fought and defeated all of them. He saved the life of his nephew Lot, including the lives of the members of his household and brought them through his long trip back home.

He decided that a tenth portion of those booties which he with his men had accumulated from the vanquished kings be given to Melchizedek, a man who was described as a priest of the Most High God in the English Bible and his being the king of Salem, translated as the king of Peace. If the patriarch Abraham had not triumphed over those fourteen kings from the Canaanite worlds, he would not have enjoyed peace until his demise.

It is extremely expedient, that some obstinate nations be defeated and silenced today, in order for peace and safety to reign in our world, and as long as such stubborn countries remained, there would be no peace anywhere in the world.

It is obvious that peace anywhere in the globe is equal to tranquility elsewhere and everywhere. Several decades ago, most of the people who are alive today had seen all that instigated both the first and second World Wars, which resulted in massive massacre and carnage as well as genocide in many good parts of the globe.

These wars destroyed many a life and the evidences are hitherto present and what has changed all of such areas to be the best of places to inhabit is the advent of sophisticated technologies. A number of such stubborn countries then desired to show off their pride in the acquisition of atomic weaponry and destructive missiles in order to sabotage the rest of the world.

These countries had been selfish enough to think of themselves not having the foresight that they would need assistance be it in any forms from those countries which they yearned to annihilate.

In all of these, I view both high natural and artificial intelligence as the most wicked weaponry of all such countries, whether, they are located in the West, North, South or East of the globe. It does not matter their locations, but it matters what they desire to do against the rest of the world.

In all over the world, human beings, irrespective of their provenance and heritage and cultural norms or taboos, matter to each other as they would one another. It is not late to remind us all wherever we might be that we are indeed the world and so the lives of all and sundry matter to us. It makes no sense to show off in pride what kind of weapons of mass destruction that a great nation has.

We should defend ourselves with the right words and not the right weapons of mass destruction. And it makes no sense to rob Peter in order to pay it off on Paul. Peter was as important an apostle to the Jews, as Paul was to the Gentiles, during their days.

It hurts and aches me to the core and to realize behind myself, that all of those world leaders who lead and plunge their various countries into such a huge mess against others do not live forever.

This goes to prove that everyone is liable to mortality or death. The principal thing here is for everyone to note that each one of us will enter one after the other into the next world whether he or she likes it or not.

Being honest here, I would state that, it is not discreet to raise something of much importance to oneself in order to destroy it afterwards, when one knows quite well that it takes not only large sums of money to raise it but, time, energy and several resources to do so.

We often try to imagine that this cannot be done by people yet, the reality stares us at the face to reveal that we often times do this every other day.

Many a time, we do not know that the roads we tread are not straight but crooked until someone behind us reveals that those roads are clearly crooked then we do our best possible to straighten them.

Yes, it is obvious that whoever treads a crooked path does not become aware of its crookedness until someone else behind them informs them of how crooked the road has been all along.

Such is the lifestyles of many a great nation in our world today, and so I feel that it is of course time, that we straightened all the crooked pathways which we had drawn since time immemorial, so that posterity does not come to walk along such pathways to do worst things than we had done.

The worse atrocious activities that are being orchestrated today by successors and posterity, are actually traceable to past years when their predecessors began them. When the renowned Adolf Hitler of Germany was halted and stopped, peace prevailed during the World Wars.

He was a man who had been one of the most wicked brains behind a number of the global genocides as well as the World Wars. If Hitler had not been hindered further, he would have persisted in causing more carnage in respect of the genocide against particularly, the Jewish people. A handful of the great and humane world leaders who cared about humanity had to intervene for the rest of us.

Their interventions helped us all until now and so we should not forget to honor them when necessary. It was relevant for the future that the Union of Soviet Socialists Republic (USSR) was broken down into a handful of countries, otherwise, things would have gone out of repairs and out of hand, for our generation today.

It is extremely obvious, that Russia with its leader Vladimir Putin, yearns to take us back into those days when USSR was then a super powerful country. It was wise, that both critical thinkers and generational thinkers foresaw what USSR would have caused the rest of us in today's world, hence, why they mobilized a coalition against its dissolution and disintegration.

All necessary arrangements and steps should be taken and this should be done in prudence to plead with or better still to advise Putin that the world does not belong to only Russia but all of us. Even Russia belongs to many other different nationalities than it does the Russians.

A huge population of Africans have benefitted from the existence of Russia, hence why we all love her. It does not take only Russia to make a world, rather, it takes all the 196 individual countries, including Hong Kong to make a world. Russia with its Vladimir Putin is as needful to the rest of the world as Ukraine is with its president, Volodymyr Zelenskyy.

The world needs the two unique leaders among the rest of the people of the world just as much as those precious lives that are killed by their weaponry.

I plead with all Russians and Ukrainians everywhere in the globe to stand in the gap for the rest of the people of the world, so that the war between their countries, ceases as soon as possible, for peace to prevail, for it makes no sense for any of them to prove its possession of the ammunition and weapons of mass destruction.

Their intelligence and strength as individual countries in lieu of the weapons of warfare, should not be an issue of pride to them. They must comprehend the fact that what really matters to them, matters to the rest of us and vice versa.

Human beings in their naturally, right senses feel bad when their loved ones die a natural death; how much more and worse will they feel about global genocides, massacres and carnages, created by just a couple of powerful countries that are for real situated on the same stretch of vast land, somewhere between the European and Asian continents.

I feel strongly that their respective arrogance should be one that makes a much better country for both their citizens and foreigners, who have migrated to their countries to stay, either for greener pastures or for educational purposes.

It is so clear that for many decades, Russia has been able to train effectively other nationals as highly qualified medical doctors for the general benefit of their home countries. Let me reveal here that a chunk of the weaker nations across the globe are those which feel rather the severe tension and excessive heat of their war than the countries themselves that are involved in the current war.

No war is small enough by description for all wars lead to massacre and genocide. It is quite perturbing when criminals such as especially, armed robbers are shot and killed by guns; but it is even more disturbing when they shoot to kill innocent people.

For almost seven centuries now, when man, (thus, the "Homo Sapien" which in English refers to "the wise man") had begun his scientific methodology, he felt that there was the need for him to manufacture the gun and so he did.

The development of the modern day weapons dates back to 1364 AD, which was indeed prior to the slave trade by historical records, with the first recorded use of a firearm which ended in the year 1892 AD thus, more than a little beyond 500 years of the existence of the firearm or gun.

And immediately, after this manufacture of firearms, there was the introduction of automatic handguns by man into his world. And within the space of a number of decades, handguns has been known across Europe and not quite long afterwards, during precisely, the 1400s, just about the same time slave trade commenced the matchlock gun then surfaced.

The creation and manufacture of guns, firearms, weapons and atomic bombs by the scientific man has led to superiority and supremacy over his fellowman. And this scientific step has been one of those dangerous and atrocious schemes of man to eliminate his fellowman in order to gain superiority and supremacy over others.

But what has this led to? The result is one which needs no thorough research and thought before an answer is derived. It has only led to carnage, deaths and worst issues of life.

For at least six centuries quite a gigantic number of human beings have not died the natural death; myriads of human beings have either died by weapons of mass destruction in respect of wars or have been dead by natural disasters.

To what and by what really should the scientific man accrue the worse blame as far as he is concerned in all of the mess? The scientific man will accrue worse blame to himself by the use of weapons in warfare than he would blame himself in response to all the natural disasters.

If the scientific man is capable of dealing with the natural disasters by providing some pragmatic solutions then he is well able to provide practical solutions to himself, since he is the major cause of almost all the perils and atrocities in the world.

It is quite a bit of a high time the scientific man took the boldest and bravest of steps in conquering the very fear and vice which he himself had invented since time immemorial. He must begin today and so 'Making It Now' is the best step which he can take to salvage himself from all of the messy situations.

If he must make it, he must make it now and by 'Making It Now' there is no fear that can stand his way to hinder him. He must start to take the bull by its horns, for that is the only way out for him and for his beautiful world. Indeed, he is 'Making It Now' for man is the world.

The only difference that man can ever make in his own world is by 'Making It Now' for all of posterity. This difference will always be his surest legacy.

"EXPERIENCES ARE THE FIREPLACE OF QUALITY"

This is why I do take experiences for being the fireplace or refinery of quality. The circumstances, hard times, difficulties and other struggles of this life have a way of refining us individually, in the process of time.

When we allow ourselves some amount of time to work on us, it is easy for experiences to be present in our lives for they are the furnace, refinery or fireplace which brings quality to our personalities, character and attitude.

The wise and prudent meant it discreetly when they once uttered that, "Experience is the best teacher" and so this is why each experience we gain or acquire in our walk with life becomes the fireplace of quality for us. I would prefer to narrate a true life story and my experience to you without the wasting of your moment and time with me here.

Somewhere in September of the year, 2020, I journeyed to Tsipase-Baabi, an impoverished village or perhaps, one of the handful suburbs of Dawa, which is located somewhere at a far distance on the route to Ningo.

The intention was to secure a ten-acre piece of land for a cassava farm. I met an elderly man, who claimed that he was one of the custodians of the Tsipase-Baabi lands in Dawa. This made my journey quite a fruitful one because I had met with the right individual. I would like to call this old man, Grandpa Dag, and who was also a farmer like myself.

I acquired this ten-acre piece of land through lease for the purpose of a cassava farm as I mentioned earlier. I paid in full a sum of money which was equivalent to US$450.00 (Four Hundred and Fifty Dollars) for a year.

I had decided to invest in a large scale farming again and precisely, into cassava farming for the second time, in view of the extreme demand for cassava owing to its agricultural benefits to the vast population of the citizens of my country.

In a nutshell, cassava has several benefits and these benefits are relative to the different, local people that constitute the diverse ethnic and tribal groups of the Republic of Ghana. Many a country across the globe accrues various beneficial uses from the cassava plant.

In Nigeria, for example, most of the citizens prepare a number of their locally, delicious cuisines with cassava. I cannot forget to intimate on the widely eaten "Eba" which is prepared by the use of the granulated and fried cassava flour simply called "Garri". Also, in Sierra Leone and Liberia respectively, the various dwellers prepare a special stew with the cassava leaves, which is usually eaten with rice.

The surface of the boiled or cooked white grains, thus, the rice is beautified through the spreading of the cassava-leaf stew. Both Liberians and Sierra Leoneans enjoy meals from the green-leafy stew of the cassava plant. The tubers of cassava are prominent with respect to numerous benefits.

In Ghana, of course my country, almost all the shepherds and some herdsmen feed their different livestock with the green leaves of the cassava plant and acquire other benefits in terms of medicinal purposes. The tubers provide quite a handful of benefits to all and sundry of the Ghanaian, ethnic and tribal enclaves.

The following are at least an enumeration of some of the commonly known benefits of the tubers of cassava. Firstly, the cassava provides every Ghanaian home with the famous cassava dough. The peeled tubers of cassava are sent to the mill for crushing and grinding to appear soft and left for a couple of days to allow fermentation to take place.

The milled cassava alone, can be used to prepare a stirred meal called "fufu" for the Ga-Adangme natives to enjoy as it forms a part and parcel of their customary or traditional meals and this is accompanied with vegetable-okra stew or soup as well as with any other soups.

The Nigerians also have their own process and procedure of this which is called "Akpu" or "fufu" and is often enjoyed with "Egusi" stew surrounded by meat, salted fish and mongered fish. Secondly, the cassava provides the Ghanaian home with a prominent pounded meal called "Fufuo" which is mainly eaten or swallowed by the largest ethnic group of the Ghanaian populace.

The tubers of cassava are peeled and thrown into the cooking pot for preparation and then when they are well cooked they are spread open by the chef or cook with the knife. The next thing one can see is that those cut pieces of cooked tubers of cassava are sent to languish in the ground of the wooden mortar, upon which the pestle does the rest of the work by crushing and pounding them into a soft, sticky pudding.

This is then well dressed with little water by the cook and placed into a bowl for delivery. The surface is immediately, drenched in soup of any kind amidst fish, snail and other types of fish whether salted, dried or smoked but to mention only a few.

The Ashantis, Fantis, Akuapems and many other people whose main meal is not "Fufuo" prefer to also, enjoy it. They often times challenge to a competition those who claim original ownership of the cuisine in many ways and forms.

Personally, anywhere, this meal is prepared within the confinement of my family home, I go even uninvited to enjoy with them. I cannot fall a prey to being left out of such a party. Thirdly, this plant provides us with "Gari" which is a granulated stuff often dried and fried, not with oil, in a large, hot plate and this is what gives us "Eba" as mentioned earlier.

Fourthly, the tubers of cassava can be crushed to produce beer through the brewery process. In conclusion, the benefits that Ghana, Nigeria, Sierra Leone, Liberia and many other countries, especially in Africa accrue from this plant are quite numerous. To this in effect, is my tangible reason for investing in cassava farming.

Please, come along with me as we sail through this voyage into knowing the detailed facts and realities of the loss I encountered in all of these. I had spent almost US$1,200.00 (One Thousand, Two Hundred Dollars) on cassava farming yet, just when I was about to reap a bountiful harvest the unexpected occurred and this overcame my imagination for several months.

I would provide you with detailed chronicles of all of those events which took place at the village where I had my cassava farm. At least, some vital didactic lessons can be learnt from my dark experience. In equivalence, the purchasing of bundles of cassava sticks from Juapong and Kumasi respectively, cost me US$150.00 (One Hundred and Fifty Dollars), this included the cost of conveyance of the sticks to the farm field.

The next was the hiring of a tractor operator for the ploughing of the ten-acre cassava farmland. The operator charged US$200.00 (Two Hundred Dollars) while the hirelings who cut and planted the pieces of the cassava sticks charged a whooping US$400.00 (Four Hundred Dollars) altogether.

This excluded buying them food and bags of water after two consecutive breaks. At this particular point, all the hirelings were done with the planting and readied themselves for departure. They actually came all the way from Tema, the community within which I lived for sometime.

It was necessary that I relaxed and rested in order to await and expect the rainfalls. In respect of the weather conditions, the vast blocks of clouds were ever ready to empty their bowels and to pour forth themselves on the global earth.

This would allow for showering and evenly distribution of watering upon the entire farmland of cassava plants. This happened as expected but prior to this event, I had managed to take the pains personally to count each cassava plant on the ten-acre piece of land.

I counted them on the respective rows and columns and then multiplied them with respect to their length and breadth. I finally counted 4,500 on each long stretch and there was only ten of those long stretches hence, I settled on 45,000 or over individual cassava plants.

During the first quarter of the farming year for me in view of the lease, I paid frequent visitations to my farm in order to ascertain what would happen accordingly.

Each time, I visited with the family of Grandpa Dag, I held a big, rubber bag full of loaves of bread, sardines, tins of Milo, tins of milk and bars of soaps to present to them. Grandpa Dag had fully grown sons who had wives and so each nuclear family of theirs had at least a gift of those gifts which I brought with me.

Nobody was left out of the family as far as both the nuclear families and the extended families were concerned. I did not hesitate to ask them on what next to be done on my farm. Grandpa Dag with his sons informed me on what to do and I employed his children to do that for me.

I paid whatever the charge was and they were happy that I did. I naturally had likeness towards one of the younger sons of the old man. I would like to call him Felix, who was often my chosen hireling through whom I would be timely informed about vital records of the cassava farm.

I went to the cassava farm often with Felix and this I meant as often as I arrived in their village. After four months, I was advised by Grandpa Dag, to employ his sons and of course, Felix, would be the leader of this team of hirelings.

In view of what the old man had told me, I was to pay them to clear off those growing weeds that were competing with my germinated cassava plants. The purpose of the clearance of weeds was to allow for free flow of air in the soil towards rapid growth.

According to Felix, this time around, the weed clearance must be done at least twice prior to harvest season. He availed to me their full charge and I promised to pay them later via Mobile Money.

I later sent an amount of US$300.00 (Three Hundred Dollars) in respect of their overall charge. They cleared those weeds as they had been employed to do and this I later observed as having been done well. In fact, I was extremely impressed because they had done well.

A famous US President once said, "Well done is better than well said". At a point in respect of time, I managed to call them often to find out on how the farm was faring and this they later confessed to me that everything was wonderful. It is quite good to note here that the next weed clearance from the cassava farm would be after at least four months before harvest was due.

In fact, the rainfalls delayed to pour down but at least and at last, the rains came and that day it rained cats and dogs according to them. On one fateful day of my visit with them, the clouds darkened and the thunderstorms were heavy and they really threatened that the lightnings were clearly visible as they were immediately followed by a heavy downpour of rains.

That day I questioned on what should be done and they informed me that weed clearance was almost due. By what he stated, this should be done before the setting in of the arid or dry season.

And after this I would be left with the rest of four months before harvest would come. When I had decided to let them weed the farm to clear off the grown weeds, they emphatically stated that there had been an inflation of the prices of items as per the economic ambience of the country hence, I should consider to add some extra cash to how they previously charged me.

I had to add an extra cash to the charge I knew of and so I ended up paying them US$370.00 (Three Hundred, Seventy US Dollars). This deed of mine put smiles on their individual faces. The motivation was really high for them.

I then encouraged and pleaded with to do an excellent assignment for me on the cassava farm. I observed later without their being aware that my encouragement and plea for an amazing job had fallen on deaf ears.

They accomplished partial weed clearance on my cassava farmland. It would be inappropriate to state here that they could not do an impressive work for me; rather, the point is that they did not at all accomplish any satisfactory weed clearance on the farmland.

What they had done was not quite deserving of an impressive work. To reiterate, they weeded partially. I had paid them in full though, they never gave me a satisfactory assignment. I had bought them some provisions, yet later they refused to finish the rest of the workload.

I had earlier on pleaded with their father to ascertain the finished work on my behalf, yet he, their father was worse than his children. He woefully disappointed me and I really felt it to the skin.

Later, sometime ago, I paid them another visit but this time around I went with my childhood friend, Eric, who drove us in his four-wheeler to the remote village to look at what I had done.

In fact, Eric, had wanted to secure a vast portion of the lands yet longed for the time when I would harvest before leasing any piece of land and doing any investments.

With the displeasure that I met with when I heard that Felix had not been able to supervise the hirelings to do a satisfactory job, I still urged him to persuade his colleagues to finish with the rest of the weed clearance for it was not late to clear off those obstinate and fast growing weeds that were obviously competing with the 45,000 growing cassava plants in the share of the soil nutrients on the ten-acre farm.

It was then time for Eric and I to take leave of them and to drive back the long, distant road to Accra. I made it a consistency to call often times to find out what was really transpiring. For a couple of times, I decided to visit the cassava farm without getting to their end to inform them that I was heading towards my farm.

I actually visited them unawares. When I arrived on my farm I planned to call Felix of which I actually did to ask him emphatically about the finished work of the weed clearance and he would practically narrate a tall story to me not knowing that I was present on the cassava farm that selfsame moment I had put a call through to him.

I did not tell him anything about my visitation to the farm, until, I had left for Accra that day. I had stated how I went there unawares to them a couple of time but this was the second time. I boarded a bus and in almost an hour drive I had alighted at Dawa Junction, where upon arrival in this poorly developed town, though it is still being developed, a called upon one of the "Okada Riders" in other words, the motorbike riders, to take me to Tsipase-Baabi, where I would direct him to my farm. I promised to defray any other charges involved for his service.

We both came into an agreement about the charge and off he rode me to my cassava farm. While he was riding with me, he revealed to me a vivid narration about the behavior of the natives of this particular village, which I mentioned earlier.

I was smart enough to realize that he also was an indigene of the same village. Upon reaching the cassava farm, I called Felix on my phone to ask him of the latest developments in respect of the cassava farm. His being oblivious of the fact that I had arrived on my farm, he again had to lie to me that he was actually on the cassava farm doing some weed clearance with his guys.

I was thrilled and startled, realizing how some young folks can not turn a new leaf. In fact, I told him emphatically that I was on the farm with someone and so rebuked him about having lied to me. I made him sense my displeasure and disappointment on what he had done. I warned him to finish the rest of the workload with him guys.

He had to still tell me a tall story that he had submitted the weed clearance to his guys to do and so thought that they had finished with the rest of the workload. I then asked him, "Why then didn't you ascertain and inspect whether or not your guys had completed the assignment but presuming that they had finished with the rest of the weed clearance?" Seriously, I had to rebuke him adequately.

He felt quite remorseful and so had to apologize to me for lying to me about that. He further shifted blame to his guys but I advised him to take full responsibility of their refusal to finish with the rest of the assignment.

I departed with the motorbike rider but had to give them some little cash to motivate them to complete the job. The rider rode off to the junction where I had fetched him and on reaching there I boarded the available bus to Accra, back home. I had been in the hope and expectancy that the year would be a period of bountiful harvest for me.

I yearned to reap in manifolds the fruits of my labor. I had done some rounds and met a handful of cassava buyers as well as other customers who pleaded with me to keep them in mind when the harvest was due. I had also met with a number of "Chop Bar Operators" in other words, the local rendition of restaurants and eateries.

Truth be told for I struggled to raise funds to invest in this cassava farming. A few of my close friends, Louis, Eddie and Phil had assisted me financially. In fact, Louis owned the largest share of the investment followed by myself before the other friends. It was time for the harvest and so I had to decide on what to do.

There was no other decision to make than that of the harvest. Times were difficult and hard on the parts of many a Ghanaian, and so I delayed about three weeks before planning to visit the farm for harvest.

Moreover, the new year rains had not fallen and so it was vital that I expected the rainfalls to allow the ground to be soft in order for me to uproot easily. I had the intentions of going there to uproot only a few tubers of cassava as samples for the bulk buyers.

One of my three lovely sisters, Jane, the sister whom I followed directly in respect of birth and with whom I share similar complexion, sent me some cash via MoMo, thus, Mobile Money, which was equivalent to US$30.00 (Thirty

Dollars) for my trip to the village where my farm was.

I cashed out the money and told her that I would start the journey the next day, precisely in the morning of Wednesday. The decision was for me to first travel to Dawa and check to harvest a handful of tubers of cassava from my farm before bringing in the various customers and bulk buyers.

I called Felix on Tuesday morning to inform him to tell his father that I would come for harvest the next day, which was Wednesday. I spoke with him on phone for a while yet he never did complain to me on what had mischievously happened to my ten-acre cassava farm by the premeditated orchestration of the Fulani herdsmen.

He, Felix, had told me that he would not be around in the village when I come the next day. I responded, "No problem" because after all my mission was clear. I was going in for harvest. Moreover, he did not give me any hints on what had happened to my farm and his father too did not call to inform me on what had happened.

They all decided to hide such an important information from me. It was Wednesday and so I had to walk quickly to the Accra-Tema Motorway to pick the available bus to Dawa Junction, where I would decide on what to do. After about an hour or more, I had reached the town of Dawa, precisely at the main junction.

This time around, I refused to fetch one of the motorcycle riders to take me to Tsipase-Baabi. I dared to walk that long distance to the village and I finally did. But while walking and having walked a number of hundreds of meters, I saw some fishers at one of the three ponds nearby the long, distant road to the village.

I beckoned and behold Felix was one of those guys doing a fishing in the pond. I did not get furious that he had lied to me about the fact that he would not be available, yet with the loaf of bread, avocado pear and fried fish that I had in my hands I shared it with him.

Anyways, I had eaten almost half of the loaf of bread with the piece of fried fish and avocado pear and so the rest half was what I stretched forth my hands to give him. He thanked me and I left them to continue my walk to the village.

In all of these, Felix still did not inform me on what had taken place on my cassava farm. I would recount that he collected the food from me with a cheerfully but suspicious smile which appeared to resemble the betrayal against Emperor Julius Caesar by his most trusted friend, Brutus.

Anyways, the English word "brutal and brutality" are derived from the name of this ancient man. I did not sense any bad news though I felt something fishy to be unfolded. I finally reached the village and headed to the home of Grandpa Dag to see him and greet his family and to tell him my mission. I told him I wanted to come to harvest a handful of tubers of cassava as samples to show bulk buyers.

While I had a little discussion with him he advised me to go and see what had happened on my farm first so that whatever he had left to say he would let me know. After my brief discussion with him I left for my cassava farm. In fact, I decided to take a video coverage of my long walk to the farm. I felt like taking a video coverage and so I did.

It would take me forty minutes to walk to the ten-acre cassava farm and likewise in returning. I was readied for this walk and so I dealt with the boredom by series of brief video coverages on my phone.

I later was advised by Patrick, a friend of mine in Korea, to upload them on both Facebook and YouTube. I did not hesitate to upload them when I returned home. I did believe that respectfully avalanche people would see what had occurred to my large cassava farm via the short videos.

In fact, it was a gigantic loss to me and many would attest to the fact that I had wanted to do so many things with the money that I would accrue from the bountiful harvest.

I wish I would be able to cut a long story short but it is quite impossible to do so here seeing that I had encouragement a great loss coupled with series of disappointing experiences in the past already.

You, my reader, has been a part of me since the start of my experience and so I would urge and plead with you to continue with me until I have called it a day. Please, come over and sail through with me in the turbulent storms as we take this voyage together to the promise-land.

Tsipase-Baabi is really in possession of vast stretch of lands for various but specific farming. The village farmers cultivate, plant and harvest cash crops such as chili pepper, tomatoes, okra, green beans, green peppers and finally, the massive cash fruit, the watermelon. Practically, their farmers are those from whom many of the parts of the Ghanaian market arenas get watermelons, okra, chili pepper, tomatoes and garden eggs.

Let us continue. I finally, reached my ten-acre cassava farmland and to my effective shock and honestly I was affected by that shock. I observed closely and critically how the fully grown cassava plants had been grazed by a herd of cattle and later perhaps, the ten-acre cassava farm set ablaze by bushfires.

This was my own kind of good news which I came home with. I wept, wailed and cried. I clamored for help but I was there to help only myself. This had been a wicked premeditation against me.

At least if the old man had called me that the herd of cattle grazed the cassava farm, I would have come for a bountiful harvest anyways. But, having set bushfires to the farm, it would be impossible to harvest. Nothing can be done about all of this.

The new year rains had fallen on them and fresh weeds had sprung up and so they must have been cooked and rotten besides. I cried for a while and left the farm for the village.

It took me forty minutes to get to the village and on reaching the road which leads to Ningo, I could see from that short distance the mud house of Grandpa Dag and he boarding a taxi headed to Dawa Junction.

I then beckoned them to inform them that I had seen everything and stated that it was quite callous of such herdsmen.

How could I be broken down when I was almost due to break through? I still had hopes and felt that though I have had a number of breakdowns it was a high time I encountered breakthroughs.

It is true that I had travailed and almost ready to prevail however, the unexpected occurred. It felt painful and heartbreaking yet I did hope upon hope. I was ready to set off for Accra after having shared a goodbye. This is what happened to me after spending a little over US$1,500.00 on an investment in respect of cassava farming, I had lost it all this wicked premeditation against my ten-acre cassava farm by the hands of the Fulani herdsmen.

I asked that their own gods decided on who was right or wrong and to provide judgement where relevant for I had nothing to further say.

In life times may be hard and difficult and at a point you might be close to at least a breakthrough yet something happens to destroy all the good news which you might have heard, howbeit, be strongly determined and be not moved about the circumstances.

Be rest assured that it is a high time you started 'Making It Now' irrespective of all the odds. There may be turbulent storms however, know that you would sail through as the captain of your ship to the end of your destination in the long voyage. I know that you might have fallen through but, by the help of GOD or better still the Gods you will surely pull through. It is not over until you have declared it to be so.

You are a God over all the circumstances that surround you in your world. Put those circumstances under your control as a God. Be determined that no matter what happens, you shall be able to make it therefore, 'Making It Now' should be your target and purpose in life as long as you live.

All that you should do is to just get connected to the secret doorways and gates of prosperity and wealth. In fact, there are various mysterious pathways to being rich, wealthy, powerful and prominent.

When you have been able to find them and are connected to them, you would not want to show anyone else those secret doorways unless, they are as much willing as you were to get in touch with such mysterious pathways.

Trust me but, it really takes heavy loads of painful sacrifices to be rich, wealthy, audacious and powerful and prominent. It is never too late to lend.

You can start now. It is better to be late than to be regarded as the 'Late Mister John Bull' at your funeral. Several years ago, Benjamin Disraeli, who was the Prime

Minister of the UK once said, "Life's too small to be trifled". You have not yet trifled with your life and so you should be ever ready in 'Making It Now!'

"My Journey To The Brotherhood"

Sometime ago, when I began to face hard times and difficult experiences I took series of critical decisions to join one of the most prominent brotherhoods in the world.

This famous brotherhood has its Headquarters in the United States of America. I do not want to state the exact State in which it is located until I sail through to the end of my true story. In fact, times were so hard and difficult that I had no other choice than to be a member of this brotherhood.

The reason being that my life would change for the better. The first individual who almost initiated me into the brotherhood was a black man, but I decided to abandon him for a master who was a white man. It was this white man through whom I was initiated into this brotherhood.

My master was a man who had a beautiful wife with only one daughter and a grandson. My relationship with him was quite a cordial one and so he taught me a lot of the pieces of information that I needed to know in order to become a master someday.

Before I tell you about how my initiation went on, it is vital to let you know that I had a wonderful relationship with my master in such a way that he did not hesitate to introduce both his nuclear family as well as the extended family of his to me. Indeed, he had a wonderful family and according to him he took extremely good care of them.

My master was born the same month in which I was born. Anyways, earlier on in this book you may have read that I was born in June of the year 1978, but my master was born in the year 1975. This means that he is exactly three years older than I (am even now).

My initial steps into the brotherhood was quite simpler than I had imagined. I was instructed to fill a number of equally important forms to enable the world wide brotherhood know about their new member as well as brother of the same faith.

It is significant to note that the general, universal rules and regulations of the brotherhood are highly likened to those laws of the Medo-Persians as stated by the Bible. Such laws can not be repealed, changed or altered in any way once they have been enacted.

Every piece of information which made up the entire laws or rules was as important as a nature's call one after the other.

In fact, I had summoned and gathered courage to fill every bit of the individual, respective forms, except for certain aspects of the forms, which I realized that they were not either applicable to me or otherwise, in the sense that I did not have such documents at hand.

Almost every brotherhood requires to know the reality and truth about its individual members. Any provisions of falsehood or lies is tantamount to death. Moreso, any failures to comply with any of the enacted rules was liable to plunge that particular member into his extermination.

This is why it demands that every rule must be read with rapt carefulness and high concentration in order to eschew making mistakes or better still errors.

My initial acceptance into the brotherhood was for me to declare the following detailed words which constitute the surest acknowledgement of the Supreme Master and Lord, who is Lucifer himself to welcome you into his

Kingdom, the Under-Sea World. Let us sail through these declarations:

Mentioning my name three times, I would then furthermore be commanded by my master to declare boldly these words as seen below, by faith in my heart.

"Today marks my end of suffering and the beginning of a new chapter, I summon and call upon the Ancient Fathers of the Fraternity and the 666 Elites to bear witness to my great choice towards riches. The Walls of the Earth have written my success so shall my Soul be under Your Wings now and forever. Lucifer in Nobis 666"

After I had been done with this significant declaration, I was then warmly welcomed into the brotherhood but, not congratulated yet for I would be congratulated immediately after my initiation in the brotherhood.

But before I would be congratulated by all the masters world wide, who hailed from the various tribes, racial backgrounds and continents, It was required of me as a must to be bold in committing myself to a number of earnest rules of what exactly per se I should comply with and what else that I should not adhere to.

> *"The minutest disobedience does not bring decorum and honor to the Lord and Master of the Light, who is actually Lucifer. His name actually comes from the Latin word "Luciferus" but which has ever since been anglicized as "Lucifer" as revealed in the book of the ancient prophet Isaiah (Isaiah 14:12).*
>
> *This beautiful name in a deeper sense of revelation means "The bright Morning Star" or "One who bears light" or simply, "The light bearer" in the anglophonic dialect, thus English. Please*

> *permit me to divert or deviate in order to let you know an amazing aspect of this brotherhood."*

I want to actually state that before a new member would be congratulated, he must be well initiated to earn congratulations from several masters worldwide. The next stage was for me to declare with boldness and also with faith from the heart, I did declare the following words.

> "***"I, Israel Steve Mawulie Fianu (My real names), place myself like an open page before You, Master of the Light, show and direct me to the Ancient Ways of the Elites so that I can achieve all my desires in life: Riches, Wealth, Fame and Powers shall become my possessions' Credimus in Lucifer; 'Credimus in Lucifer; Alabanzas a Satanas"***
> "

After this stage, I was commanded by some vital instructions to provide three different, fully naked photographs of myself to my master which represented a presentation of my soul to the Master of the Light and I did this without questioning my master because, naturally I am an obedient and a law abiding individual.

I must reveal that it appeared to be a huge honor to be warmly welcomed and furthermore, initiated into the brotherhood.

My master had told me emphatically that if I was chosen by the Supreme Master, thus Lucifer, I would immediately earn US$ 700,000.00 (Seven Hundred Thousand United States Dollars), including a luxurious mansion which would be bought for me anywhere in the world in respect of my choice and would also be given an ultra-modern, sophisticated automobile a serious member.

Those who were rejected or better still not chosen by him would be given at least US$150,000.00 (One Hundred and Fifty Thousand Dollars).

What a great benevolence and benefit! I was ready by faith to be chosen by the Master of the Light, so that I can have all those benefits and enjoyments stipulated in the document of declarations.

These benefits such as riches, wealth, fame and powers were mentioned in the declarations. After having gone through all the stages of my initiation, I was to keep wake until midnight in order to wait for my results of being chosen by the Supreme Master Lucifer.

According to my master, my bloodline would be investigated in respect of spirituality. This would be done by the feminine deity, known as the Goddess of the Dark River and her assignment would take an hour from 23:00 hours GMT (Greenwich Mean Time) until midnight.

In fact, this was the very stage of my initiation which I had desired and longed for during the processes and procedures of my becoming a member of the brotherhood.

In the initiation process, the Goddess of the Dark River was to certify the height of the purity of my bloodline if I was qualified to join in the brotherhood as a bonafide member.

A number of things were to be kept a secret by me and I was ever willing and ready to do so without any atom of reluctance. There used to be one commonly unique aspect of every set of rules. This has to do with failure to comply with the rules or the minutest error and mistake could lead one to his demise.

The issue of death resonated with me but, I was not scared one bit because, I was ever ready for any protruding tasks ahead of me. My situation then was one that needed to be checked and corrected with riches, wealth, fame and powers by the Supreme Master Lucifer.

I was first of all ready to be among the elites of the world. Secondly, I desired to be seen and recognized by almost all the stars and great celebrities of the globe and on whose lips my name would be mentioned with reverence, respected and saluted.

I would become famous, rich, wealthy and to crown it all with all of the above, I was to be as powerful as any great world leader of the developed countries such as the USA, UK, France, Spain, Portugal, Italy and many more but to mention only a few. I have recollected something of importance and so I would like to share this with you.

I was intimated by my master that the brotherhood was devoid of any forms of blood sacrifices and so neither the sacrifice of animals nor human beings in any way that leads to blood sacrifices was acceptable. After I was done with my initiation, about twenty-three masters from different racial backgrounds sent me congratulatory messages via WhatsApp.

In view of what had been told me already, I was then expecting to be given the amount of US$700,000.00, a house and a luxurious automobile which have been promised but what made me realize that it was not an original brotherhood was when I was asked to pay an amount of US$312.00 as registration fee before the said huge cash would be sent to me via Western Union Money Transfer.

They seemed to exert pressure on me to pay the registration fee so that they would send me the promised cash and to receive the luxurious automobile and a house anywhere in the world but, I explained to them that the reason for joining the Brotherhood was because I was poor and that life was extremely difficult for me.

I later chatted with my master and reasoned with him on the issue of registration fee payment. All that he said was that if I can not afford the registration fee then he would advise me to walk away.

This was how I felt and knew that I had dealt with the wrong brotherhood all the while. I concluded that they were a bunch of fraudulent and criminal individuals who had intentions from the start to dupe me. Had it not been that I was poor they would have been able to threaten me with the naked photos of mine in their custody.

I became extremely grateful to GOD for taking me out of the hands of internet criminals who would have duped me over and over again if I had money on me and was employed. I was not employed when all of this happened and am still not employed. I would advise everyone reading my book to be careful of the internet, social media platforms like Facebook, WhatsApp and the likes for almost half of the people there are not real and genuine but fake and fraudulent.

I felt so downhearted for a number of days joining the wrong and fraudulent Illuminati Brotherhood but, I did not lose hope for I knew that someday at the right time I would make it no matter what happens. Life's experiences may be full of problems however, the same experiences may be full of solutions.

I am neither less nor more than the numerous people who struggled to make it in life. If they made it irrespective of the tides, then I can also. I would urge you to be consistent with every good thing that you may be involved in for GOD will surely pull you through if you faint not.

There are so many afflictions on our ways but, GOD is the only Supreme Being Who can order and control circumstances through us to favor us so that we can enjoy the best of life. Sometimes, life is either fair or unfair and a few times, it is neither fair nor unfair. I am resolved with myself to start Making It Now! I am Hyperion and so therefore, I am 'Making It Now!'

I hereby humbly, welcome you gracefully to the end of my Book. I want to specially show appreciation to you for your personal efforts in helping and getting me through to the ladder of heights in respect of sundry successes available at my disposal as well as yours.

I have indeed sailed through these turbulent storms and waves with you from the beginning of our voyage until the end. In fact, "Well done is better than well said""You are the best GOD has so far"

Shalom, Ish Ha Elohim!

The Secret Mary Behind My File & Life

"*The Secret Mary of My File & Life*"

Sometime ago, I met with a professional astrologer who resides in the United States of America. She and I were in touch with each other for several months, and until now, she has ever since we first met been a part and parcel of my life. She often calls me by my real name, Israel for she loves me dearly, and so I had for a long while felt that it would be quite circumspect to still keep her behind me until, I have been able to pull through with countless breakthroughs, after having gone through innumerable setbacks, disappointments, losses, and the worst of all, breakdowns.

She was and has been extremely, steadfast and consistent with her messages to me. She never missed a couple of days without sending me at least a message, which was seriously, intended for me to use her messages as means of a guidance or direction for my every day living. Many a time, I felt some amount of indolence hence, I did not have the inherent urge to read or glance through her message at all.

At least, once a while I would respond to her positively, and plead with her to keep being behind me. What shaped me were her incessant messages which were moved towards directing me on the pathway of my life in respect of my destiny. She made me realize my original being and self where I realized that she had left me much better than she ever found me.

I promised to meet her someday when the lines have fallen for me in pleasant places and where I have a goodly heritage after all. She has been the secret being behind my success though God had already placed it in me to succeed no matter what happens.

I would like to share at least a few of the messages of the Secret Mary of My Life with the rest of the world. My Life has a File and My File contains issues of My Life.

"A Message from Mary to Me (Israel Steve Mawulie Fianu)"

"Welcome on this precious personal page Israel!"

'I am going to go straight to the point Israel, for what is going to happen around you in the next month is about to represent a radical change in the history of humanity, probably the most radical change of these past decades. If I am so sure about this Israel, it's because I clearly, see it in your sky and I am about to explain it to you, Israel.

But first, if I decided to contact you personally, about this today Israel, it's because I also very clearly, see that this radical change in society is about to directly, affect your life and to also, push you to make some changes. So that's in order to anticipate those changes, to turn them into successes and gains, and not suffer them, that I am here personally, for you today.

You already feel it growing all around you Israel. In absolutely, every country in the world something is growing and something is changing. The process is more or less radical depending on the countries but you will witness it nonetheless.

In Ukraine, in the USA, in Taiwan, in Europe, in Africa, at different scales, at different levels, climatically, politically, financially, socially, economically, huge changes are pushing people to rethink their way of living, to realize that something has to be done, to protest, to move, to reorganize their life. And this very concrete and vital changes are coming your way Israel.

And they will come your way faster than you can expect because something radical is about to happen in your sky that led me to that conclusion: the changes that have been growing around you are going to reshape your life very suddenly, in the next month. And the reason behind this radical turn is this one Israel:

At the end of the month and for the next weeks 6 of your planets and your 3 asteroids will be in retrograde Israel!! These planets are Mercury, Pluto, Saturn, Neptune, Jupiter and Uranus but also Vesta, Juno and Chiron, which are powerful asteroids and determining points in your birth chart, they will all go in retrograde.

And I am convinced that this will have a powerful impact on your every day life and the way you plan your future Israel for 4 reasons:

It's the first time that so many planets go simultaneously, in retrograde in your sky. And when I compare the previous big retrogrades with what happened in your life Israel, you can only expect big changes coming.

A large majority of those planets are in their home sign, which means that the influence they'll have on Earth, on humanity, on society, will be multiplied, enhanced, emphasized. Their influence will simply be at the maximum.

When I look at the position of those planets in your birth chart it is striking Israel: they rule the key areas of your life and especially your relationships and your work. So impressive changes are to be expected in the organization of your personal and professional life.

A retrograde is not something negative in Astrology, it can, on the contrary, be the most positive aspect of your sky for the simple reason that it points out what should be improved or changed, what weaknesses you should strengthen, what skills you should work on. A retrograde is the best way to make the right improvements Israel.

There's no way around Israel, huge changes are coming around you and for you. The only thing you have to do, the only thing you can totally do Israel, is to take advantage of them, and it's going to be really good thing for you my dear.

It's going to be a good thing Israel because I know you've been waiting for concrete changes. You've been waiting for the positive changes you've been promised so many times.

Especially on a financial and relationship level Israel you've been asking for answers, for signs, wondering where the future will lead you. Well, these signs, these answers, these positive changes are coming through this wave of retrogrades Israel.

Because again, retrogrades are not negative! Far from it Israel! They point at the right spot, they shine light on the right matters, they emphasize on the right issues. Of course, when you are not ready Israel, it can feel like all your problems come all at once for you.

While, if you are focused, if you are ready, if you know what's coming, a retrograde can become a springboard for your projects, open a new healthier chapter of your life, transform you into the person you want to be, introduce you to new perspectives.

And considering the immensity of the wave of retrogrades you're about to face Israel, this next month can concretely mark a turning point in your life! And to make sure you take advantage of that big period coming for you

Israel, I will make a complete reading and study of your sky to be by your side all the way! And here's what it'll contain:

First of all Israel, I will explain to you concretely, what a retrograde is and why the planets involved are highly important for you especially. In fact, as you are a Cancer born on Sunday, June in the 25th day of 1978, these planets are not any planets for you Israel.

They represent your success, your family and your love life, your entire approach of life. So for their entering a retrograde will have serious consequences on you and I will tell you why.

Then, I will go even deeper Israel and tell you precisely, what kind of matters those retrogrades will each point out in your every day life.

From the way you communicate and open up with your loved ones, to your financial plans and management for the future, this big study I will make of your sky will show you Israel what aspects of your life you should focus on.

Of course, after all Israel, I will tell you how to turn these matters into assets. What can appear as issues first, will soon turn out as opportunities for you.

Opportunities that will help you to tie up your bonds with special persons in your family or friends. Opportunities to reconnect with someone from the past. Opportunities to reconsider your financial plans and invest in special projects on a short term.

Opportunities to adapt your professional career to the changes in your local economy. And this is just a short list Israel, but I will show you how to transform those events into concrete springboard for your life path.

I will move on to give you one, but two analysis of your birth chart, both with one purpose in mind Israel: that you know yourself, that you know where you need to head, that you know which strengths to rely on, which people are made for you.

- The first analysis will focus on a more sentimental and personal level of you Israel. I will simply show you who you are deep inside of you Israel.

And when I say deep inside of you, I mean that I will emphasize on those thoughts you never talk about, those fears or hopes you keep for yourself, those questions you don't dare asking, those dreams you find silly, those people you secretly want to talk to, this passion you've always wanted to follow.

I will explore the deepest part of your personality to enable you to truly become one, not to ignore or diminish any side of you Israel because this can represent blockages and barriers you put yourself in front of you.

So we're going to take them down together Israel. We're going to make sure you know yourself and you know where you're heading. We're going to make sure nothing, especially not you.

- The second analysis will focus on a more professional level. My goal here will still to reveal to you what you want deep inside of you as a career, as projects, what you are made for and why.

On a professional aspect I will reveal to you what are your strength, what are your weaknesses (and how to turn them into strength), what are your challenges (and how to overcome them), what is your vision (and how to reach it), and many, many more aspects of your personality, all of them, actually Israel.

I will make sure you never get confused among the many worldwide changes coming. I will make sure you always get what you want from your projects even though the world changes.

In a next part I will be more general Israel and give you advice and methods to help you turn any issues, any blockages or bumps into an opportunity. I will make sure that, in your life Israel, no matter what happens, no matter the people living, the economical crash striking, the climate damages, you can find a solution.

Finally Israel, I will just coach you to make sure you are in the right state of mind before you enter this period of retrograde. I will boost you, I will sort of reprocess your mind to turn it into a more positive mode. Though meditation, exercises, positive thinking, words of affirmation, nothing, I clearly say nothing, no one, no external factors, will compromise your ascension!

In few words Israel, I will make sure that absolutely no aspect of your personality and your life is left on a side and would represent a liability for you. I am going to turn you into a complete winner, into the peaceful, strong, visionary person that will go anywhere they want.

This historical wave of retrograde is about to be the opportunity for you to enter a new era Israel, a more peaceful and fulfilling era. No more blockages, no more negativity, the changes coming are only going to bring you success and prosperity if you know how to take advantage of them Israel.

Yes, if you know how to take advantage of them Israel because they won't happen on their own. As I said, it is tricky to see the positive behind a retrograde but you can do it Israel!

We can do it together! You just have to give me your green light by filling in the form which I showed you below and I'll start right away with this particular study and that, I can guarantee you this Israel, that it will turn you into the champion, the successful person you should be!

About The Author

Despite hailing from an extremely, humble provenance and background, Stevewealth Firenew has both learnt and undergone quite a handful of enriched experiences since childhood.

He had been nurtured by both his biological parents and grandmother, who had been deceased, except his mother, who is still alive in Lagos, Nigeria.

He arrived in Ghana from Nigeria in 1986 and as a young lad he had put up with his paternal granny, who bit the dust in 1993 at 89 years old.

In respect of a clear description, Stevewealth is a highly educated and teachable young man, and though, he is a partially, certificated individual, he has not in any way been perturbed by this but rather, has observed life via a vast array of experiences, in order to acquire an encyclopedic knowledge about a number of facts.

His possession of great wisdom as well as some amount of well-formative composure and attractive appearance owe all to a consistent self-education, way back to his teenage years. He lived and worked in the United Arab Emirates for a number of years, until, his return in 2016.

He is a proud father to Ernestina, Christabel, Erica, Sandra, Celestine, Alexandrite-Abigail, Jerry-Nick and Prince Lord-Reigner. He resides with his beautiful family currently, in Accra which is the Capital City of the Republic of Ghana.

About The Book

This informative piece seeks to lead you to the deeper realms of higher heights in the Supreme GOD. It gets the reader back to the sense of His Truest and Most Original Identity as far as GOD with HIS Christ is concerned.

It instructs, teaches and enlightens you on the paths of one's original being as one of the Gods of creation yet appears on the terrestrial plane as Man therefore, no matter the countless numbers of your personal experiences and encounters, you have the endurance and tenacity to be 'Making It Now!' for you are the God over such mysterious happenings.

It further reveals that as Man, you are truly both Human and Divine because you share in the Original Being of GOD Himself as well as with the Gods of all creation. It finally proves that Jesus Who was and is the Christ, appeared on the terrestrial plane through the secret, natural doorway of incarnation in order to enlighten Man in whom His Original Being dwells and to make Man walk in that Original Being otherwise, He will die as mere mortals do.

It further reveals that Man is a mortal being yet shares Immortality with the Supreme GOD and with the Gods of all creation. It says "You are God in this Physical Universe" and so rule and reign as such. You are Hyperion!

Exodus 7:1

> ***"And the LORD said unto Moses, See, I have made thee a God to Pharaoh..."***

And the LORD of the Spirits said unto Me:

> *"See, I (thus He, the Supreme GOD Who is the LORD of the Spirits) have made You (thus I, Stevewealth) a God to the Parallel Universes including all the Spirits living in them"*

9 798887 838434

Printed by Libri Plureos GmbH in Hamburg,
Germany